The Cold War

# IN THIS SERIES

*General Editors: Eric J. Evans and P. D. King*

LANCASTER PAMPHLETS

# The Cold War

## 1945 –1991

### *John W. Mason*

London and New York

First published 1996
by Routledge
11 New Fetter Lane, London EC4P 4EE

Simultaneously published in the USA and Canada
by Routledge
29 West 35th Street, New York, NY 10001

Reprinted 2000, 2002

*Routledge is an imprint of the Taylor & Francis Group*

Typeset in Bembo by
Ponting-Green Publishing Services, Chesham. Buckinghamshire
Printed and bound in Great Britain by
TJ International Ltd, Padstow, Cornwall

*British Library Cataloguing in Publication Data*
A catalogue record for this book is available from
the British Library

*Library of Congress Cataloging in Publication Data*
Mason, John W.
The Cold War, 1945-1991/John W. Mason
p  cm. – (Lancaster pamphlets)
Including bibliographical references.
1. Cold War.   2. World politics – 1945–
I. Title    II. Series.
D843.M256   1996
909.82-.dc20     96-7549

ISBN 0-415-14278-4

# Contents

# Foreword

Lancaster Pamphlets offer concise and up-to-date accounts of major historical topics, primarily for the help of students preparing for Advanced Level examinations, though they should also be of value to those pursuing introductory courses in universities and other institutions of higher education. Without being all-embracing, their aims are to bring some of the central themes or problems confronting students and teachers into sharper focus than the textbook writer can hope to do; to provide the reader with some of the results of recent research that the textbook may not embody; and to stimulate thought about the whole interpretation of the topic under discussion.

# Preface

The cold war was a period of intense antagonism between the two superpowers – the United States and the Soviet Union – lasting from 1945 to 1991. Because there was no direct armed conflict between the two continental giants the description 'cold war' remains an accurate one. Now that it is over, and we know the outcome, it is tempting to re-define this period of recent history as the 'long peace'.

The cold war began in Europe with the division of Germany and the establishment of the Soviet empire in Eastern Europe in 1945. It ended with the break-up of that empire in 1989, the re-unification of Germany in 1990 and, finally, the collapse of the Soviet Union itself in 1991. In the middle of this 45-year period the cold war spread around the world to Asia, Africa, the Middle East and Latin America. This book focuses less on the global dimension of the cold war than on the particulars of the Soviet–American relationship since 1945.

Two points gave the Soviet–American relationship its particular flavour: ideology and nuclear weapons. Among other things the cold war was a propaganda war: each side proclaimed its ideology in an uncompromising, absolutist way. The Soviet Union believed for a long time that communism could only triumph after a war had destroyed capitalism. The United States believed that communism in the Soviet Union would have to collapse before there could be lasting peace in the world. By the logic of their respective ideologies, therefore, the two superpowers were set on a collision course.

But the cold war was also coterminous with the first nuclear age. Nuclear weapons are absolute weapons, qualitatively different from the weapons of all previous times. One Trident nuclear submarine, for example, carried more fire power than all the bombs dropped in the Second World War.

The United States and the Soviet Union clumsily engaged in a dance of death, threatening one another with weapons that they knew must never be used. The danger of nuclear war hung over the cold war like a poisonous cloud of extinction, making it a period of history like no other. It is a history about what did not happen as much as what did happen. I hope this book conveys something of this dimension of the cold war.

I am indebted to the work of a number of scholars – all from the United States – who have made major contributions to our understanding of the cold war. I should like to single out for mention the following authors whose ideas have had a strong influence on my own: George Kennan, Louis Halle, Raymond Garthoff and J.L. Gaddis.

J.W.M. 1996

# List of abbreviations

| | |
|---|---|
| ABM | anti-ballistic missile |
| ARVN | Army of the Republic of South Vietnam |
| CIA | Central Intelligence Agency (USA) |
| CND | Campaign for Nuclear Disarmament (UK) |
| Cominform | Communist Information Bureau |
| FNLA | National Front for the Liberation of Angola |
| GDR | German Democratic Republic |
| ICBM | inter-continental ballistic missile |
| INF | intermediate-range nuclear forces |
| KMT | Kuomintang (Nationalist Party, China) |
| MAD | mutual assured destruction |
| MIRV | multiple independently targetable re-entry vehicle |
| NATO | North Atlantic Treaty Organization |
| NSC | National Security Council (USA) |
| SALT | Strategic Arms Limitation Talks/Treaty |
| SDI | Strategic Defense Initiative |
| SEATO | South-East Asia Treaty Organization |
| SLBM | submarine-launched ballistic missile |
| START | Strategic Arms Reduction Talks/Treaty |
| UN | United Nations |

# Chronology

**1945**

| | |
|---|---|
| February | Yalta Conference |
| May | Germany surrenders – end of Second World War in Europe |
| June | UN Charter signed |
| July/August | Potsdam Conference |
| August | Atomic bombs dropped on Hiroshima and Nagasaki; Japan surrenders |

**1946**

| | |
|---|---|
| February | Kennan's Long Telegram |
| March | Churchill's 'Iron Curtain' speech |

**1947**

| | |
|---|---|
| March | Truman Doctrine |
| June | Marshall Plan announced |
| October | Cominform set up |

**1948**

| | |
|---|---|
| February | Communist *coup* in Czechoslovakia |
| June | Berlin Blockade begins |

**1949**

| | |
|---|---|
| April | North Atlantic Treaty signed |
| May | Berlin Blockade lifted |
| August | Soviet Union explodes atom bomb |
| September | Federal Republic of Germany (West Germany) established |

| | |
|---|---|
| October | German Democratic Republic (East Germany) established |
| October | People's Republic of China proclaimed by Mao Zedong |

**1950**

| | |
|---|---|
| February | Sino–Soviet Treaty of Friendship signed |
| June | Outbreak of the Korean War |

**1952**

| | |
|---|---|
| November | US explodes H-bomb |
| November | Eisenhower elected president |

**1953**

| | |
|---|---|
| March | Death of Stalin |
| July | Korean armistice signed |
| August | Soviet Union explodes H-bomb |
| September | Khrushchev becomes First Secretary of the Soviet Communist Party |

**1954**

| | |
|---|---|
| April | Geneva Conference on Korea and Indo-China |
| May | Fall of Dien Bien Phu |
| September | SEATO established |
| December | US and Taiwan sign Mutual Defence Treaty |

**1955**

| | |
|---|---|
| April | Bandung Conference of Asian and African nations |
| May | West Germany joins NATO |
| May | Warsaw Pact established |

**1956**

| | |
|---|---|
| February | Khrushchev denounces Stalin at the 20th Congress of the Soviet Communist Party |
| October | Hungarian uprising |
| October | Suez crisis |

**1957**

| | |
|---|---|
| October | Soviet Union launches an earth satellite – Sputnik |

**1958**

| | |
|---|---|
| November | Khrushchev Note on future status of Berlin |

**1959**

| | |
|---|---|
| January | Castro overthrows Batista in Cuba |

**1960**

| | |
|---|---|
| May | Paris summit breaks up |

| August | Soviet technicians withdrawn from China |
| November | Kennedy elected president |

**1961**

| April | Bay of Pigs landing |
| August | Berlin Wall built |

**1962**

| October | Cuban Missile Crisis |

**1963**

| June | US–Soviet Union sign Hot Line agreement |
| August | US, Soviet Union and Britain sign the Nuclear Test Ban Treaty |
| November | Kennedy assassinated; Johnson becomes president |

**1964**

| October | Khrushchev replaced by Brezhnev |
| October | China explodes first atomic bomb |

**1965**

| February | US begins bombing of North Vietnam |

**1966**

| April | Cultural Revolution begins in China |

**1967**

| June | Six-Day War in Middle East |

**1968**

| January | Tet Offensive in South Vietnam |
| October | Brandt becomes West German Chancellor |
| November | Nixon elected president |
| November | SALT talks begin |

**1970**

| August | Soviet–West German Treaty of Non-Aggression signed in Moscow |

**1971**

| September | Quadripartite Agreement on Berlin signed |
| October | People's Republic of China admitted to the UN; Taiwan expelled |

**1972**

| February | Nixon visits China |
| May | Nixon visits Moscow; SALT I signed |
| December | East and West Germany sign Basic Treaty |

**1973**

| January | US–Vietnam armistice signed |
| October | Arab–Israeli (Yom Kippur) War |

**1974**

| | |
|---|---|
| August | Nixon resigns as result of Watergate scandal; succeeded by Ford |
| November | SALT II outline agreed by Brezhnev and Ford |

**1975**

| | |
|---|---|
| April | Vietnam War ends |
| August | Final Act of Helsinki Declaration signed |
| November | Angola becomes independent; beginning of civil war |

**1976**

| | |
|---|---|
| September | Death of Mao Zedong |
| November | Carter elected president |

**1977**

| | |
|---|---|
| February | Marxist coup in Ethiopia led by Mengistu |

**1979**

| | |
|---|---|
| January | US and China establish diplomatic relations |
| June | Brezhnev and Carter sign SALT II |
| December | Soviet Union invades Afghanistan |

**1980**

| | |
|---|---|
| August | Birth of Solidarity under Lech Walesa in Poland |
| November | Reagan elected president |

**1981**

| | |
|---|---|
| December | Martial law imposed in Poland |
| December | US imposes economic sanctions against Poland and the Soviet Union |

**1982**

| | |
|---|---|
| June | START negotiations begin in Geneva |
| November | Death of Brezhnev; succeeded by Andropov |

**1983**

| | |
|---|---|
| March | Reagan announces SDI |
| November | NATO deploys cruise and Pershing missiles in Europe |

**1984**

| | |
|---|---|
| February | Death of Andropov; succeeded by Chernenko |

**1985**

| | |
|---|---|
| March | Death of Chernenko; succeeded by Gorbachev |
| April | Gorbachev announces freeze of Soviet missile deployments |
| November | First Reagan–Gorbachev summit in Geneva |

**1986**

| | |
|---|---|
| October | Reagan–Gorbachev summit in Reykjavik |

**1987**

December    Reagan–Gorbachev summit in Washington; INF Treaty signed

**1988**

November   Bush elected president

**1989**

January     Cuban troops leave Angola

February    Soviet troops withdraw from Afghanistan

June        Solidarity wins Polish parliamentary elections

October     Hungarian Communist Party dissolves

November   Berlin Wall collapses

December   Non-communist government takes power in Czechoslovakia

December   Ceauşescu's government overthrown in Romania

**1990**

October     East and West Germany reunite

**1991**

January     Beginning of the Gulf War

July        Bush and Gorbachev sign START I

August      Attempted *coup* against Gorbachev

December   Gorbachev resigns as president of the Soviet Union; the Soviet Union formally disbands

# 1

# The origins of the cold war in Europe, 1945–9

### 1917: The historical roots of Soviet and American foreign policy

The year 1917 was a momentous one in the history of the twentieth century. It was the year when the two great extra-European powers – the Soviet Union and the United States – stepped into the mainstream of history to proclaim two rival world ideologies. The United States, under President Wilson, entered the First World War not to restore the balance of power but to end the whole European state system and 'make the world safe for democracy' under a new international order. Russia, under the leadership of Lenin, had the Bolshevik Revolution, withdrew from the war and called for a 'world' revolution. There is a sense, ideologically speaking, in which it is accurate to speak of the cold war beginning in 1917. The full impact of these two events, however, was not to be felt until after 1945, when political power moved from the centre of Europe to Moscow and Washington.

There are three main sources of Soviet foreign policy. First is the historical experience of Tsarist Russia before 1917. Since the seventeenth century Russia had been subject to attack and invasion, especially from the West, and therefore always felt insecure. Second, after the Bolshevik Revolution of 1917 Russia dropped out of the First World War and was subsequently

1

invaded by the Western allies in the years 1918–20. Churchill spoke of 'strangling Bolshevism in the cradle', which confirmed the Soviet leaders' belief that the West was aiming at the capitalist encirclement of the Soviet Union. Third, the Soviet Union was inspired by the ideology of Marxism-Leninism, which predicted the collapse of capitalism. But as Lenin declared, before the collapse, 'a series of terrible conflicts between the Soviet Republic and the bourgeois states is inevitable'.[1]

If the Soviet Union always felt weak and insecure, the United States, by contrast, felt safe and aware of its strength. The historical experience of the United States was that of isolationism. But when Japan attacked Pearl Harbor in December 1941 and brought the United States into the Second World War, President Roosevelt revived Woodrow Wilson's language of universalism. He defended United States policy in terms of the abstract principles of democracy and economic freedom (later enshrined in such documents as the Atlantic Charter (1942) and the Declaration of Liberated Europe (1945)). The high-sounding moral rhetoric of American foreign policy infuriated the Soviet Union, but it happened to reflect the United States' long-term economic interests. Roosevelt called for an economic policy of the 'Open Door' – free trade and equal access to raw materials – in order to prevent a relapse into the Depression of the 1930s.

Both the Soviet Union and the United States, then, wanted security after 1945, but each defined it in a different way. The Soviet Union was still a regional power after 1945 and security for it meant 'friendly' states on its border. The United States was a global economic power and security for it meant a world open to the free exchange of goods, money and people.

## The breakdown of the Grand Alliance in 1945: Yalta and Potsdam

On 22 June 1941 Nazi Germany attacked the Soviet Union with 270 divisions in the greatest land war in history. United States public opinion was still isolationist. But when Japan attacked the United States naval base at Pearl Harbor (7 December 1941) and Hitler declared war on the United States three days later, the latter joined Britain and the Soviet Union in the Grand Alliance. Almost immediately the problem of setting up a second

2

front in Western Europe came to dominate the Alliance.

The second front came in June 1944, but by then the Soviet Union had already borne the brunt of the war against Germany, suffering losses estimated at a ratio of fifty Soviet soldiers killed for every one American. Whatever the reason for the delay in setting up the second front, it was to have far-reaching consequences for the post-war political settlement. The West had to try to win at the conference table what it had forfeited on the battlefield. The West's primary objective was to defeat Hitler, but it also feared the intrusion of Soviet power into Eastern Europe. The key country here was Poland.

Poland was the country over which the Second World War had broken out when Germany invaded it in September 1939; likewise, Poland was at the centre of the origins of the cold war after 1945. In October 1944 the Soviet Union allowed the pro-Western Warsaw uprising to be crushed by the Nazi occupation forces. It was now becoming clear that the Soviet idea of 'friendly' governments in Eastern Europe clashed with America's long-term interests.

In an attempt to reach some agreement on their outstanding differences, the Big Three (the United States, Soviet Union and Britain) met for a week at Yalta in the Crimea in February 1945. At Yalta it was agreed to divide Germany into four zones of occupation and have the Soviet Union enter the war against Japan three months after Germany's defeat. But the most important issue was Poland. Stalin recognised only the communist-based Lublin Polish Government; at the same time he signed the Declaration of Liberated Europe, which called for Eastern European governments 'broadly representative of all democratic elements . . . and free elections of governments responsible to the will of the people'.[2]

Did Roosevelt really believe that the Soviet Union would honour its pledge to hold free elections in Poland and the rest of Eastern Europe? If he did not, he kept such thoughts to himself and led the American people to believe that no fundamental differences existed between the Soviet Union and the United States. It was a fatal misjudgement. Stalin had no problem squaring the ideal with the real. The Red Army occupied Poland and no paper declarations could remove it. Stalin's view was clearly expressed to the Yugoslav Milovan Djilas in April 1945: 'this war is not as in the past: whoever occupies

3

territory also imposes his own social system as far as his army can reach. It cannot be otherwise.'[3]

Roosevelt died on 12 April 1945 and Vice-President Harry Truman took over the presidency. Some historians have seen the transition from Roosevelt to Truman as the moment when the cold war began. But there is no evidence to show that Truman was intent on reversing Roosevelt's policy towards the Soviet Union. No solution had been found to the Polish question. No agreement had been reached on the future shape of the United Nations Organization. In May 1945, however, Truman abruptly ended Lend-Lease aid to the Soviet Union.

The Big Three met for their last conference of the war at Potsdam, outside Berlin, in July 1945. The German question dominated the sessions: agreement was reached on the need for the joint occupation and demilitarisation of Germany, but the issue of reparations brought out fiercely opposing views. A complicated agreement was finally reached whereby the Soviet Union would take reparations from its own zone of occupation and also receive 25 per cent of all machinery and industrial plant from the Western zones. In return, the Soviet Union would send to the Western zones food, coal and raw materials to the value of 60 per cent of what it received from the West. The agreement began to unravel within a year.

### 'Atomic diplomacy' – Hiroshima and after

One week after the Potsdam Conference, on 6 August 1945, the United States dropped the first atomic bomb on Hiroshima. The effect of the bomb on United States diplomacy towards the Soviet Union and the origins of the cold war has been the subject of heated controversy among historians. Gar Alperovitz, in his revisionist work *Atomic Diplomacy*, claims that Truman's hard-line attitude towards the Soviet Union was the direct consequence of America's possession of the bomb.

Alperovitz argues that the United States dropped the bomb on Japan mainly as a demonstration of its military power to the Soviet Union and, subsequently, was able to use it as a diplomatic lever to wring concessions from the Soviet Union in Eastern Europe. It is true that Truman began to take a harder line against the Soviet Union in the autumn of 1945, but this was mainly owing to Republican pressure in Congress. At the same time the United States began to demobilise, reducing its forces from 12 million to 3 million in one year, and this weakened its bargaining power.

At the London Conference of Foreign Ministers in September 1945 the United States refused to recognise the puppet governments of Romania and Bulgaria. But there is no evidence to suggest that Stalin's foreign policy was influenced by the United States' possession of the bomb. Indeed, Adam Ulam suggests that the United States' early monopoly of the bomb (the Soviet Union acquired the bomb in August 1949) actually weakened United States foreign policy by inducing a sort of Maginot psychology. 'Like a miser with a treasure', Ulam writes, 'so America hugged the evanescent atom monopoly to its bosom, equally unable to exploit it or to exchange it for something useful.'[4]

The conditions for the creation of the cold war were set in the Second World War out of disagreements among the Big Three about what kind of post-war settlement should be made in Europe and the Far East. Each side acted according to its own historical dictates: when Germany collapsed in May 1945 their very different visions of the future shape of Europe and the world stood revealed. The cold war was not the product of one event or decision – it was the result of a fundamental clash of ideologies and interests between the Soviet Union and the West.

## Eastern Europe: cockpit of the cold war, 1945

The immediate origins of the cold war lie in the conflict between the Soviet Union and the West over Eastern Europe. At Yalta Churchill declared that, for Great Britain, the fate of Poland was a question of honour. Stalin replied that, for the Soviet Union,

> it is not only a question of honour but also of security . . . not only because we are on Poland's frontier, but also because throughout history Poland has always been a corridor for attack on Russia. . . . During the last thirty years our German enemy has passed through this corridor twice. . . . It is not only a question of honour but of life and death for the Soviet State.[5]

What Stalin said about Poland was true to a lesser extent of the other Eastern European countries. He therefore insisted that their governments be 'friendly' towards the Soviet Union, which in practice meant not allowing free elections.

By contrast, United States interests in Eastern Europe were abstract and idealistic. The United States was thousands of miles away and traditionally had little trade with the area. It must be remembered that most of the states of Eastern Europe – Finland, Estonia, Latvia, Lithuania, Poland, Czechoslovakia, Hungary, Romania, Bulgaria and Yugoslavia – were created after the First World War out of old dynastic empires according to the principle of national self-determination proclaimed by President Woodrow Wilson. In 1945 Roosevelt was determined to have a just and lasting peace settlement based on the principle of a people's rights to choose their own form of government and where they wanted to live.

Roosevelt placed great hopes on the establishment of the United Nations Organization (April 1945) and this is crucial to an understanding of his wartime diplomacy regarding Eastern Europe. It meant that all decisions about territorial changes were postponed until after the war – a course of action virtually amounting to a 'policy of no policy' towards Eastern Europe. Meanwhile, the future of Eastern Europe was being predetermined by the advance of the Red Army and Stalin's training of East European Communist Party leaders to take over their governments.

When the Red Army occupied the entire pre-war territory of Poland in January 1945 the pro-Soviet Lublin Committee was installed as the provisional Polish government and free elections never took place thereafter. Within two years of the end of the Second World War, Soviet-style communism had spread to eleven states in Europe with a combined population of over 100 million people: Latvia, Estonia, Lithuania (all directly annexed by the Soviet Union), Poland, the eastern zone of Germany, Czechoslovakia, Hungary, Romania, Bulgaria, Yugoslavia and Albania. The success of the Soviet Union in expanding its political and social system into Eastern Europe led to widespread fears in the West that in 1946 and 1947 perhaps Greece, then Italy, and even France would be the next to fall.

## 1946: an 'iron curtain' descends on Europe

1946 is a neglected year in histories of the cold war. It stands between the more dramatic years 1945 (the year of the Yalta and Potsdam Conferences) and 1947 (the year of the Truman Doctrine and Marshall Plan). Yet there is a strong case for dating the beginning of the cold war as 1946.

Iran was the site of the first direct confrontation between the Soviet Union and the West after 1945. It was the British at first rather than the Americans who were concerned about whether the Soviet Union would end its occupation of northern Iran after the war. When the Soviet Union refused to withdraw its troops within six months of the end of the war (as agreed by the Anglo–Russian–Iranian Treaty of 1943) Truman's Secretary of State, James Byrnes, urged the Iranian Prime Minister in February 1946 to resist further Soviet advances into the region. This marked a fundamental shift in United States policy. In the words of Fraser Harbutt, it reflected 'the beginnings of a profound geopolitical change that would rapidly take the United States for the first time into the heart of the Anglo–Soviet confrontation in the eastern Mediterranean and the Near East'.[6] Thereafter, the United States assumed responsibility for preventing undue Soviet influence in the region.

In the same month, February 1946, Britain's former prime minister Winston Churchill delivered his famous 'Iron Curtain' speech in Fulton, Missouri. He set out to depict the Soviet Union as an expansionist state and to change once and for all the Yalta attitudes and policies of accommodation towards the Soviet Union. The threat from the Soviets lay not in military expansion, he argued, but domestic subversion. Churchill's call for an Anglo–American alliance to meet the Soviet challenge was premature, but his speech marked an important shift away from Yalta.

1946 was also the year when Moscow and Washington failed to agree about control of the atomic bomb. The Baruch Plan recommended the establishment of an international 'Atomic Development Authority' run by the United Nations, which would control all uranium deposits to be used for peaceful purposes only, but leave the United States with the right to continue to manufacture its own atomic bombs. Not surprisingly, the Soviets rejected the Baruch Plan, which would have left the United States with a permanent monopoly of atomic power.

In the same month as Churchill's iron curtain speech, the United States *chargé d'affaires* in Moscow, George Kennan, sent an eight-thousand word telegram to the Truman administration in Washington. The effect of the famous Long Telegram was sensational – copies were circulated around the Pentagon and it became 'the bible for American policy-makers'.[7] The Soviet Union, Kennan wrote, did not believe that peaceful co-existence was possible between the communist and capitalist world. At the bottom of the Kremlin's neurotic view of world affairs, Kennan wrote, was 'an instinctive Russian sense of insecurity which, combined with Marxist dogma, made Soviet expansionism more dangerous and insidious than ever before'.[8]

The implications of Kennan's analysis were chilling: if Soviet foreign policy was formulated not as a response to what happened in the outside world but only as a result of conditions within the Soviet Union, then no action taken by the United States would diminish Soviet hostility towards the West. The policy Kennan recommended can be summed up in one word – 'containment'. Containment was essentially a policy of the middle way, between isolationism on the one hand and preventive war on the other. It was adopted as the official policy of the Truman administration in 1947.

## The Truman Doctrine and Marshall Plan, 1947

United States foreign policy was in a state of confusion in early 1947. As we have seen, the United States began to take a more aggressive stance towards the Soviet Union in 1946. But Congress was dominated by Republicans intent on reducing military spending and no one knew how to gain diplomatic advantage from the nuclear monopoly. Public opinion was not convinced of the Soviet threat. Truman had little room for manoeuvre but his chance came with the crisis in Greece in 1947.

In February 1947 the British Government delivered two notes to the United States State Department announcing its intention to suspend all economic and military aid to Greece and Turkey after 31 March. How would the Truman administration respond? Dean Acheson, the Secretary of State, described in his memoirs, *Present at the Creation*, his meeting with Congressional leaders at the White House:

8

These Congressmen had no conception of what challenged them; it was my task to bring it home. . . . In the past eighteen months, I said, Soviet pressure on the Straits, on Iran and on northern Greece brought the Balkans to the point where a possible breakthrough might open three continents to Soviet penetration. Like apples in a barrel infected by a rotten one, the corruption of Greece would infect Iran and all to the east. It would also carry infection to Africa, through Asia Minor and Egypt and to Europe through Italy and France, already threatened by the strongest domestic Communist parties in Western Europe.[9]

We can see here an early expression of what was later called the 'domino theory' – a theory that was to dominate and plague United States foreign policy for the next generation and provoke fierce debate during the Vietnam War.

In order to win Republican support for aid to Greece and Turkey, Truman had to couch his request to the American people in terms of an ideological confrontation between democracy and communism. The result was his speech to Congress on 12 March 1947, announcing what became known as the Truman Doctrine. Truman referred to every nation as having to choose between two ways of life and declared that it was the policy of the United States 'to support free people who are resisting attempted subjugation by armed minorities or by outside pressures'.[10] With these words Truman, in effect, wrote a blank foreign policy cheque that could be cashed in by any country in the future that demonstrated it was in danger of a communist threat. The Truman Doctrine was proclaimed in the universalist language of a crusade to support 'free people' everywhere: it set the tone and substance of United States foreign policy for the next two decades.

At the time of the Truman Doctrine Western Europe was in a state of severe economic crisis. The new Secretary of State, George Marshall, responded with a plan for massive United States aid for Europe. The Economic Recovery Programme (the official name of the Marshall Plan) supplied grants and credits totalling $13.2 billion to sixteen European countries.

The Marshall Plan was an obvious economic success. By 1952 Europe's industrial production had risen to 35 per cent above the pre-war level. An answer was found to the problem of reviving the German economy, without allowing German domination, by linking Germany to a European-wide recovery plan. To humanitarians the Marshall Plan brought long-term aid to a Europe in economic chaos. To those in the United States who feared a slump in exports and a lapse into depression, it offered a way to revive world trade. To those who feared communist subversion in Western Europe it provided the means to create healthy national economies that would win over the working classes to their liberal capitalist regimes.

The very success of the Marshall Plan caused a crisis in Soviet–Western relations. The Soviet Union, not surprisingly, refused to participate and its subsequent denunciation of the plan sealed the economic and political division of Europe. By the spring of 1948 Europe was divided into two distinct economic and political blocs, one dependent on the United States, the other dependent on the Soviet Union. The Soviet Union's response to the Marshall Plan came in September 1947 with the establishment of the Communist Information Bureau (Cominform). The Cominform was an odd institution whose main task was propaganda – to keep the communist parties in Europe subservient to Moscow and to proclaim the Soviet way as the only true road to socialism.

Another aspect of the new militant Cominform policy was to speed up the consolidation of Soviet controls in Eastern Europe, a process that culminated in the *coup* in Czechoslovakia in February 1948. By the end of 1948, non-communist leaders in Poland, Hungary, Romania, Bulgaria, Yugoslavia and Albania had been eliminated by terrorism, faked trials and political purges. Czechoslovakia was different from the other countries in Eastern Europe – it was the one country that might have been able to reconcile a Western-style democracy with the requirement of being 'friendly' to the Soviet Union.

But in late 1947, when the economic situation in Czechoslovakia began to deteriorate, the communist Minister of the Interior filled key police posts with trusted comrades and prepared trials against political opponents. When the non-communist members of the government resigned in protest, President Benes installed an all-communist government in February 1948. The Czech *coup* 'sent a shock wave through the civilised world'.[11] The events in Prague helped win public support for Truman's containment policy. The United States Congress, for example, endorsed the Marshall Plan by an overwhelming majority two months later.

## The German question, the Berlin Blockade and NATO, 1948–9

The last, and most important, phase of Stalin's rejection of the Marshall Plan was the Berlin Blockade of June 1948. In order to understand the problem of Berlin it is necessary to grasp the crucial importance that Germany played in the deterioration of relations between Moscow and Washington from 1945.

The four victorious allies (the United States, the Soviet Union, Britain and France) agreed at the Potsdam Conference that occupied Germany should undergo the 'five Ds': demilitarisation, de-industrialisation, decentralisation, democratisation and denazification. Germany was to be divided into four zones of occupation, but to be treated as a single economic unit through the Allied Control Council (ACC), with its headquarters in Berlin. Berlin itself, which lay 110 miles inside the Soviet zone, was divided, similarly, into four zones to be governed by an Allied Kommandatura reporting directly to the ACC.

Germany's geopolitical position in the centre of Europe, coupled with its industrial potential, made it the crucial country in the European and even global balance of power. Lenin's dictum 'Whoever has Germany has Europe' still held true. But because of the total collapse of Germany in 1945 each occupying power had the opportunity to mould its zone in its own image. The result was that Germany came to be divided politically and economically as well as militarily.

The first breach between the Soviet Union and the West over Germany came in 1946 when the complicated reparations agreements between the Soviet and Western zones broke down. The Western response was to merge the British and American zones into Bizonia in January 1947. There was strong pressure in the West to revive Germany economically and integrate the three Western zones into the European recovery programme. This was precisely what the Soviet Union feared. Such a state, containing three-quarters of the population of Germany, as well as its old industrial heartland (the Ruhr and Rhineland-Westphalia), might serve as a focal point of attraction to Germans living in

11

the Soviet zone. Even more alarming to the Soviets was the possibility that a West German state closely allied to the United States might one day become a military power again and threaten the Soviet fatherland.

On 24 June 1948, one day after the Western powers introduced a new currency in the Western zones, the Soviet authorities cut off all passenger and freight traffic to West Berlin. The Berlin Blockade had begun. From the Soviet point of view Berlin was an ideal place to demonstrate a show of strength. Buried deep inside the Soviet zone, West Berlin's 2.4 million inhabitants were at the mercy of the Soviet occupation forces. Legally, the West had failed to secure written confirmation of its rights of access by land to its sectors of the city. The Americans and British responded to the Soviet challenge by a massive airlift that supplied the beleaguered citizens of Berlin with food, fuel and other basic commodities for almost a year. The round-the-clock missions to Berlin caught the world's imagination and cast the Soviet Union, portrayed as trying to starve women and children, in a bad light.

In May 1949 Stalin acknowledged the failure of the blockade and ended it. Berlin was the first open conflict between the two cold war antagonists. Yet it did not lead to a hot war. The United States did not use its nuclear monopoly to break the blockade; the Soviet Union did not use its conventional military superiority to force the West out of Berlin. Soviet restraint was probably influenced by the fact that the United States had transferred sixty B-29 bombers, capable of carrying nuclear bombs, to British bases at the height of the crisis.

The Soviet Union imposed the blockade on Berlin in response to the introduction of a currency reform in the Western zones of occupation. But the real reason was an attempt to prise the Western Allies out of Berlin and prevent the setting up of a pro-Western German state. The conflict over Berlin went beyond a diplomatic clash and had all the characteristics of a war. But the United States' possession of the bomb made it a conflict with a difference. The existence of nuclear weapons revolutionised classical military strategy for the first time, reducing the options open to each side. Neither side took advantage of its particular form of military strength. Berlin was the first conflict in the nuclear age to show the strong tendency on both sides to freeze the geographical *status quo*.

The events in Europe in the late 1940s culminating in the Berlin Blockade made it clear to West European leaders that only the United States could ensure the balance of power in Europe. Ernest Bevin, the British Foreign Secretary, saw the need to bring the United States into a Europe shattered by the collapse of Germany and the emergence of a well-armed Soviet Union. The North Atlantic Treaty, signed in Washington in April 1949, provided the answer.

The purpose of NATO was in fact psychological. The strategic concept on which the common defence of Europe was based was simple – the ability of the United States to deliver the atomic bomb. By throwing a nuclear cloak over their half of the continent the West Europeans were given a secure basis on which to work towards economic recovery and resistance to internal communist subversion. No attempt was made to rectify the imbalance of army divisions on each side of the Iron Curtain, estimated to stand at about 125 to 14 in favour of the Soviets in 1949. This was the dilemma at the heart of NATO. Because it was politically unable to build up Western European ground strength to match that of the Red Army, NATO had to rely on the bomb to deter a Soviet attack. The United States' nuclear guarantee was to remain the keystone of the alliance.

# 2

# Communist China and the cold war in Asia, 1945–53

At 4.00 a.m. on the morning of 25 June 1950 North Korean armed forces launched a devastating attack on South Korea and within hours had crossed the 38th Parallel. This began the Korean War, which lasted over two years until a final cease-fire on 27 July 1953. It has been the only conflict since 1945 in which the armies of two great powers – the United States and China – met on the battlefield. The Korean War transformed relations between the United States, the Soviet Union and China in Asia and froze them into a cold war mould for the next two decades.

The Korean peninsula itself occupied a sensitive, strategic point bridging China and Japan; but in 1950 it was an obscure, politically divided, economic backwater from which both the United States and the Soviet Union had withdrawn their occupying forces in the previous year. In order to understand why the Korean War played such a crucial role in shaping East–West relations, it is necessary to examine two related events: the triumph of communism in China in 1949; and the United States' attempt to apply the policy of containment to Asia.

## Mao Zedong and the triumph of communism in China, 1949

In 1911 the Chinese nationalists, led by Sun Yat Sen, overthrew the Manchu dynasty and set up a republic. Thereafter, China

14

was in a state of chronic civil war, as no government was able to establish its rule over more than part of the country. After the death of Sun Yat Sen in 1925 a dominant faction emerged, the Kuomintang (KMT), or Nationalist Party, led by Chiang Kai-shek.

When Japan attacked China in 1937, beginning the war in the Far East, Chiang and the KMT became a key ally to the Americans in the war against Japan. After 1945 President Roosevelt saw China as an obvious choice to become one of the 'Four Policemen' (along with the United States, the Soviet Union and Great Britain) to protect world peace. But what Roosevelt never realised was that the United States had allied itself to a corrupt, decaying government that, despite huge injections of American money and weapons, was losing the support of the Chinese people. There was a strong Chinese lobby in the United States that saw Chiang and his American-educated wife, Madame Chiang, as great leaders of a 'free China'. The influential press magnate Henry Luce, publisher of *Life* and *Time* magazines, placed Chiang Kai-shek's portrait on his covers more times than any other world leader in 1945.

One journalist who wrote for *Time–Life* publications was T.H. White, who was sacked by Luce when he refused to gloss over the darker side of Chiang's rule. He returned from China to write *Thunder Out of China*, which became an instant best-seller in 1946. White's eye-witness experience of the Honan famine in 1943 had convinced him that Chiang's regime was doomed. Chiang Kai-shek's regime had failed both to resist the Japanese and to tackle China's appalling domestic problems of poverty and corruption. White wrote later:

> Had I been a Honan peasant I would have acted as they did when, a year later, they went over to the Japanese and helped the Japanese defeat their own Chinese troops. And I would have, as they did in 1948, gone over to the conquering Communists.[1]

The Chinese Communist Party (CCP) was founded in 1921 by Mao Zedong and a small group of followers. After Chiang massacred thousands of communists in Shanghai in 1927, Mao and his force of 100,000 troops set off on the legendary 'Long March', the survivors ending up in the north-western province of Shensi.[2] From there the communists engaged in guerrilla

15

action against Japan and in the process built up a large, peasant-based army. By 1945, when the Japanese surrendered, the communists had almost a million troops, occupied one-quarter of China and governed almost 100 million people.

How can one explain the reversal of fortunes of the communists and nationalists in the period 1937 to 1945? One clue to the answer can be found in the different way that each responded to the Japanese invasion of China. From 1937 Japan occupied the eastern third of China, stretching from Beijing to Canton. The KMT strategy was to withdraw to the remote western headquarters of Chunking on the Yangtse river and trade space for time. Chiang was more concerned with the enemy within than the enemy without: 'The Japanese are a disease of the skin, the communists are a disease of the heart', he once said.[3] Chiang failed to win over the peasants in villages because he was unwilling to introduce land reform for fear of alienating his support among the landlords. Further, he refused to fight the Japanese. This meant that it was the communists, not the nationalists, who emerged as the most enthusiastic patriots. Paradoxically, it was nationalist sentiment rather than communist ideology that won the communist party its popularity.

The communist revolution in the countryside went virtually unnoticed by American political leaders. For American public opinion China automatically meant Chiang and the KMT; the Chinese Communist Party was either ignored or seen as part of the Soviet-inspired world conspiracy. This profound misreading of events in China was to have a catastrophic effect on both Sino–American and Soviet–American relations.

The surrender of Japan on 14 August 1945 brought the Second World War to an end and set the stage for a bloody civil war in China. The KMT forces, with massive United States aid, seized most of the cities in the north, while the communist guerrilla forces gained control of the countryside. In an effort to forestall civil war President Truman sent General Marshall to China in December 1945 to try to get the KMT and CCP to agree to a cease-fire. Marshall's attempt to mediate between the two sides broke down one year later, partly because the United States still continued to supply aid to the KMT.

United States policy towards China over the next few years was summed up in Dean Acheson's phrase 'letting the dust settle'. The early advantage enjoyed by the KMT over their communist opponents, in both numbers and equipment, was soon squandered. Morale was poor among the KMT troops and the officers alienated the population by taking public property and land for their own personal use. By 1948 the military initiative had passed to the communist armies in Manchuria and North China. Marshall, who was now Secretary of State, refused to meet the Nationalist Government's request for an increase in military supplies and declared that the United States would only support Chiang 'for so long as he was supportable'.[4] By 1949 that time was past. The KMT retreated to the off-shore island of Taiwan (Formosa) and the new communist government was formally proclaimed by Mao Zedong in Beijing on 1 October 1949.

The so-called 'loss' of China sent shock waves across the United States. Even before the triumph of Mao the Truman administration had come under strong attack for being 'soft' on communism. Truman's administration was the victim of its own success in selling the doctrine of containment in Europe to the American public. From 1947 to 1949 the Truman Doctrine, Marshall Plan and NATO had stopped any further communist advances in Western Europe. Chiang Kai-shek's many supporters inside and outside Congress asked why communism was not so vigorously resisted in China. The Truman administration never answered this question convincingly and thus left itself vulnerable to endless carping from its critics.

The 'loss of China' debate in the United States was not allowed to die down, though it often had little to do with events in China itself. In the presidential election of November 1948 Truman won a surprise victory over his Republican opponent, Thomas Dewey. The Republicans, bitter at being excluded from office since 1933, ended their support for Truman's foreign policy. In August the Soviet Union exploded an atomic device, ending the American atomic monopoly and changing the strategic outlook dramatically.

In February 1950, the same month that the new communist regime in China concluded an alliance with the Soviet Union, a junior senator from Wisconsin, Joseph McCarthy, declared in a speech in West Virginia: 'I have in my hands 57 cases of individuals (in the State Department) who would appear to be either card-carrying members, or certainly loyal to the Communist Party, but who nevertheless are helping to shape our foreign policy'.[5]

The Republicans now had an issue that could bring them back to power after twenty years – 'twenty years of treason', as McCarthy called it. The domestic ramifications of the McCarthy witch-hunts need not concern us here. In foreign affairs Mc-Carthyism had two consequences, one specific, one general. First, by pointing the finger of blame at the Far Eastern Division of the State Department for the 'loss' of China, McCarthy's attacks drove a whole generation of China experts out of the State Department, leaving it bereft of expertise in a vital area of foreign policy. Second, McCarthyism forced the Truman administration on the defensive and made it extremely difficult for the President to prosecute a 'limited war' in Korea when large sections of the population were calling for total victory.

### The Korean War: the 'Pearl Harbor' of the cold war

After the defeat of Japan in 1945 Korea was divided at the 38th Parallel, with the Soviet Union controlling the north and the United States controlling the south. By 1948 North Korea was a well-established communist state under the leadership of Kim Il Sung, and the Soviet Union accordingly withdrew its troops. South Korea, led by Syngman Rhee, felt anxious in the face of North Korea's superior armed strength. Nevertheless, American forces withdrew in June 1949 and Dean Acheson declared South Korea to be outside the United States' 'defensive perimeter' in the Pacific in January 1950.

The world was taken by surprise when North Korean forces crossed the 38th Parallel in June 1950. Historians are not agreed about who really instigated the North Korean forces to attack the South.[6] China could not have had any motive for unleashing a war in Korea. The CCP was concerned with domestic economic problems and, in any case, Mao would not have wanted to support any action that would strengthen Kim Il Sung, who was an ally of the Soviet Union, not China.

What part did the Soviet Union play in the North Korean attack? Most Western observers at the time took the view that Kim Il Sung was no more than a puppet of Stalin and that the attack on South Korea was masterminded by the Soviet Union. More recent evidence has pointed to the key role played by Kim Il Sung in instigating the war. The US historian Bruce Cumings claims that Kim Il Sung acted in June 1950 not on Stalin's orders but out of a deep nationalist conviction to unify the country and revolutionise the south.[7]

It still remains a mystery, in the light of what we know about the disastrous effects the Korean War had on Soviet–American relations, why Stalin sanctioned the attack. He was normally very cautious in his foreign policy and, while he would have preferred to see Korea ruled by a communist regime, the unification of the whole peninsula by the north cannot have been a priority for him. We know that he did not want a major crisis in Korea and was careful not to become too involved in the conflict. This is shown by the fact that he decided one week after the war began to withdraw all Soviet pilots and advisors from North Korea in order to avoid the danger of a Soviet commitment.

The United States' response to the North Korean attack was immediate and decisive. The issue was taken to the UN Security Council, who condemned the attack by a 9–0 vote. This was an odd, one-off decision, made possible by the fact that the Soviet Union had boycotted the Security Council since January 1950 over the refusal to allow the Chinese People's Republic a seat. The absence of the Soviet Union gave the United States a great opportunity to bring in the moral authority of the UN to back up US action.

The United States possessed the advantage of acting in response to a case of clear-cut aggression that all the world could see. This was no gradual, confused Stalinist take-over in Eastern Europe, where it was impossible to determine what had really happened. The aggressor and victim stood out clearly – it was Pearl Harbor all over again.


## The Korean War and its consequences in Asia and Europe

President Truman appointed the Second World War hero General Douglas MacArthur as Commander of UN forces in Korea. In the early months of the war MacArthur drove the North Korean forces out of the South in a series of brilliant counter-offensives. In October 1950 MacArthur was given a free hand to carry the war north of the 38th Parallel. This in turn provoked China to send its own forces across the Yalu River into Korea. By the end of November nearly 300,000

Chinese troops had driven UN troops into a long retreat that was halted just south of the 38th Parallel.

The Truman administration was faced with a dilemma. General MacArthur called for the use of atomic bombs against China to stem the flow of troops into Korea. Rumours that the United States might use atomic weapons in Korea sent the British Prime Minister, Clement Attlee, rushing to Washington to voice his opposition to their use. Further, it was generally assumed (wrongly, as it turned out) by Washington that the Chinese had acted under Soviet instigation, and there was an ever-present fear that a direct attack on China would automatically bring in the Soviet Union under the terms of the Sino–Soviet Alliance of February 1950.

Once the Truman administration had opted for a limited war, MacArthur's position – which rested on all-out victory – became untenable. In April 1951 Truman sacked MacArthur. The man who had been called the 'American Caesar' returned home to a hero's welcome but the United States' allies heaved a sigh of relief. The removal of MacArthur was significant in the cold war because it ended the main challenge to the idea of limited war and the doctrine of containment.[8]

It is too often forgotten that the earlier decision to cross the 38th Parallel was made not by the military but by the civilians Truman and Acheson. Four-fifths of all American casualties in the Korean War occurred after the UN forces crossed the 38th Parallel. It is convenient to blame the military, especially MacArthur, for the United States' problems in Korea, but all the main decisions were made by the President and Secretary of State. Still, Truman stuck to his conviction, in the face of hostile public opinion, that Korea was not the place to fight an all-out war against communism. MacArthur's policy of using nuclear weapons, even if militarily feasible, would have damaged, perhaps irreparably, the United States' political credibility and moral standing in the world.

The Korean War dragged on for another two years, with neither side gaining a decisive advantage. Soon after he took office as President in January 1953, General Eisenhower warned China indirectly through the Indian ambassador that, unless progress was made at the peace talks at Panmunjom, the United States would consider using the atomic bomb against China. It is impossible to know what effect this message had. In March

1953 Stalin died and in July 1953 a cease-fire agreement was signed that set the demarcation line between North and South Korea just north of the 38th Parallel.

The Korean War has been described as 'the century's nastiest little war'.[9] 'Little' is a relative term. The United States lost 33,000 killed and missing, 105,000 wounded. South Korea lost 415,000 killed and 429,000 wounded. It is estimated that more than 1.5 million Chinese and North Koreans died. Within the peninsula itself the war sealed the division between North and South and left a legacy of great bitterness and tension between the two countries.

Outside Korea the effects of the war were momentous. Before the war NATO was merely a statement of intent; after the war it was a full military alliance. Before the war Truman had refused to implement a famous policy document (NSC-68) issued by the State and Defense Departments, calling for a tripling of United States defence expenditure, in order to meet the Soviet threat anywhere in the world. After the outbreak of the Korean War Truman did just that: in 1951 he increased the defence budget to $50 billion, compared to $13.5 billion of six months earlier. In 1952 plans were drawn up to increase the number of NATO divisions from fourteen to fifty and agreements were made to set up bases for American ground, air and naval forces in Europe. As a result of the Korean War, United States military power was injected right into the heart of Europe.

The consequences of the war were no less dramatic in the Far East. The war brought with it the extension of the cold war to the entire Pacific rim. In addition to South Korea, where United States military forces remained, the United States concluded a treaty with the Philippines (August 1951) re-affirming air and naval base rights there and agreeing to its defence. In September 1951 a tripartite security pact was signed by the United States, Australia and New Zealand (the Anzus Pact) whereby the United States took over Britain's traditional role as protector of the area.

The most important addition to the United States' zone of defence in Asia was Japan. The United States' military occupation of Japan, like its occupation of Germany, was originally designed to prevent the defeated nation from ever again threatening the security of its neighbours. But the Soviet–American

21

confrontation prompted Washington to re-build the Japanese economy as fast as possible, so that it would not be a tempting target for communist subversion. The Korean War transformed Japan from an impoverished enemy into a prosperous ally and made the United States appreciate its value as a counterweight to Soviet and Chinese power in the Far East. In September 1951 the United States and forty-eight other nations signed a peace treaty with Japan. On the same day Washington and Tokyo concluded a security pact allowing United States military forces to stay indefinitely and providing for a major base on the island of Okinawa.

The effect of the Korean War on the Nationalist Government of Chiang Kai-shek in Taiwan was to tie it more closely to the United States. Economic and military assistance was resumed to Chiang's government in exile and continued throughout the 1950s and after. The United States' Seventh Fleet remained in the Taiwan Straits, interposed between the mainland and Chiang Kai-shek's regime. In 1954 the United States went one step further and concluded a treaty of mutual defence with Taiwan. The Nationalist Government of Chiang, not the communist Government of Mao, continued to be recognised by most non-communist countries as the 'Republic of China' and kept its seat in the United Nations. The Korean War froze Sino–American relations into a state of hatred and mutual incomprehension for the next two decades.

It is almost impossible to exaggerate the impact of the Korean War in shaping the course of the cold war. The Korean War abruptly ended the incoherence of American foreign policy in the years 1946–50. By 1951 all the characteristics we have come to associate with the cold war were present – high defence budgets, a militarised NATO, the emerging Sino–Soviet bloc and the belief that the world was so closely interconnected that a communist victory anywhere would threaten vital US interests.

The Korean War was also important in setting a precedent for fighting a limited war in the nuclear age. President Truman's dismissal of General MacArthur in April 1951 established the idea that 'victory' need not be the only aim of military policy. The Korean War was the first important war in recent American history that was not a crusade, in the sense that the goal was not the physical destruction or ideological transformation of the enemy. The Korean War was Truman's war, not MacArthur's: it was a limited war, not a total war, and to that extent reflected the realities of international politics in the nuclear age.

# 3

# Peaceful co-existence and nuclear confrontation, 1953–64

## Eisenhower, Dulles and the 'New Look' defence policy, 1953–8

Eisenhower's Republican presidency (1953–61) is often presented in text-books as marking a radical break in foreign policy between the Democratic administrations of Truman (1945–53) and Kennedy (1961–3). Under the trigger-happy Secretary of State, John Foster Dulles, notorious for his spine-chilling phrases – 'massive retaliation' and 'brinkmanship' – the United States is portrayed as being led to the brink of nuclear war in defence of some obscure, peripheral area in Asia. The reality is quite different. Eisenhower and Dulles continued to apply the containment policy, though with a change of emphasis and style. What made the difference to the Eisenhower administration was the experience of the Korean War. The frustrations caused by fighting an unwinnable war in Korea cast a long shadow over United States foreign policy in the 1950s.

During the election campaign of 1952 Dulles spoke out against the 'negative, futile and immoral policy of containment which abandons countless human beings to a despotism and godless terrorism'.[1] Both Eisenhower and Dulles promised a policy of 'liberation' of the people in Eastern Europe. Reacting against the Korean War experience, the Republican administration promised a 'New Look' defence policy that emphasised the United States' commitment to use nuclear weapons whenever it was thought appropriate.

The Republicans, as the party of big business, were keen to reduce taxes and balance the budget, mainly by reducing defence expenditure. At the same time they wanted a more aggressive foreign policy. The way out of the dilemma was to rely overwhelmingly on strategic nuclear power. In the phrase of the day, this policy would provide 'a bigger bang for the buck'.[2]

But, as so often with United States foreign policy, the rhetoric was at odds with the reality. An examination of three conflicts in the early years of the Eisenhower presidency – Korea, Indochina and the Taiwan Straits – will reveal how far a policy of 'liberation' and 'massive retaliation' had replaced containment.

We have seen that Eisenhower used the threat of nuclear weapons to persuade China to sign an armistice in Korea. Yet he remained very sceptical about their use. The South Korean President, Syngman Rhee, hoped to unite his country with the help of the United States. When he suggested this to Eisenhower in 1954 he got a stern lecture on the nuclear danger. Eisenhower replied: 'War today is unthinkable with the weapons which we have at our command. If the Kremlin and Washington ever lock up in a war, the results are too horrible to contemplate. I can't even imagine them'.[3]

In Indochina (comprising Laos, Cambodia and Vietnam) France was fighting a war against the Viet Minh, who sought independence from colonial rule. The origins of what later became the Vietnam War will be examined in Chapter 4. Here we need mention only the role played by the United States in 1954. By that year the United States was paying two-thirds of the French expenses in Indochina. In a desperate effort to crush the Viet Minh forces in open battle the French set up a garrison of 15,000 of their best troops in Dien Bien Phu. When it became clear that they had walked into a trap and could not win, the French called on the United States for military support.

The president ruled out sending ground troops from the start. 'This war in Indochina would absorb our troops by the division', he told the National Security Council, prophetically, in January 1954.[4] Admiral Radford and the Pentagon then recommended 'Operation Vulture', which would involve the use of three tactical nuclear weapons, thought to be sufficient to smash the Viet Minh at Dien Bien Phu. But Eisenhower was not prepared to use nuclear weapons. Further, he would not act without Congressional support and, even more important, would not intervene without the support of Washington's allies. Britain was the key ally and its prime minister from 1951 to 1955, Winston Churchill, made it plain that his country opposed any military intervention in Indochina. On 7 May 1954 Dien Bien Phu fell. The 'New Look' strategy clearly was not applied in Indochina.

The third test of the 'New Look' strategy came in 1954 and 1955 over the Taiwan Straits. In preparations for a military invasion of Taiwan, Communist China repeatedly shelled the two tiny islands of Quemoy and Matsu, lying just off the coast of China but belonging to the Nationalist regime of Taiwan. Admiral Radford and the Joint Chiefs of Staff recommended using atomic bombs against the mainland. Again, Eisenhower rejected the nuclear option on the grounds that it would be impossible to limit such an action.[5] All three crises – Korea, Indochina and the Taiwan Straits – show that in practice Eisenhower departed from Truman's strategy only in appearances. Despite the rhetoric of 'massive retaliation', the policy pursued was one of self-deterrence.

Eisenhower's presidency was dominated by the search for peace. Three days before he was elected in 1952 the United States exploded the first hydrogen bomb in the Pacific. The explosion was nearly 1,000 times larger than that of the bomb used to destroy Hiroshima. In an age when one United States bomber carried more destructive power than all the explosives set off in the entire world's history hitherto, Eisenhower was acutely aware of the need to inform the American people of the realities of the nuclear age. In 1953 the Soviet Union exploded its first hydrogen bomb in Siberia.

In the 1950s the Soviet leaders were very much aware of the awesome firepower of thermonuclear weapons. Behind all the cold war rhetoric they recognised the United States' reluctance to use the bomb. What has to be explained is how and why the years of 'peaceful co-existence' in the mid-1950s were abruptly ended and followed by an era of nuclear confrontation between the two superpowers, culminating in the Berlin and Cuban crises of 1958–62.

## The 'thaw' after Stalin's death, 1953–6

The death of Stalin on 5 March 1953 threw the Soviet governing elite into disarray. There was a big power struggle within the collective leadership, with no single individual strong enough to dominate Soviet foreign policy. During this interregnum, led by Malenkov and Molotov, an attempt was made to relax tension with the West. In 1955 Khrushchev emerged as the leader.

Over the next decade, until his overthrow in 1964, Khrushchev was to become world famous as the architect of de-Stalinisation and the doctrine of 'peaceful co-existence'; but his motives and behaviour have never really been understood in the West. The same man who called for 'peaceful co-existence' with the United States brought the world to the brink of nuclear war in the Berlin and Cuban crises. It has too often been assumed without question that Khrushchev's anti-Stalinism automatically made him a kind of liberal advocate of détente with the West. This view is mistaken, as will be shown below.[6]

Khrushchev believed that the situation in Europe had become stable and that the Soviet Union could therefore relax its grip on non-essential areas, such as Austria and Finland, whilst maintaining the socialist camp by every possible means. In 1955 the Soviet Union withdrew from Austria – which had been under Four-Power occupation, just like Germany – on condition of Austria's permanent neutrality. In the same year the Soviets returned to Finland the Porkkala naval base taken at the end of the war. The Geneva summit of 1955 achieved little of substance, but it marked the end of the Soviet Union's long isolation in world affairs. The 'spirit of Geneva' became the popular phrase of the day.

Khrushchev's most dramatic break with the past came in his 'secret' speech to the 20th Party Congress in February 1956 denouncing Stalin. He brought in a new era in Soviet foreign policy by revising Lenin's dogmas on war, capitalism and revolution. He rejected Lenin's thesis that war between capitalism and communism was inevitable; in a nuclear age he called for the 'peaceful co-existence' of both camps. Within the socialist camp Khrushchev allowed for different 'national roads to socialism'. There is a direct link between this speech and the uprising in Hungary later in 1956.

When riots broke out in Poland in June 1956 the Polish

Government restored order itself without recourse to Moscow and even elected Wladyslav Gomulka, a symbol of nationalist communism who had been jailed earlier by the pro-Soviet puppet regime, as First Secretary of the Party without consulting Moscow. The Soviet Union did not intervene militarily in Poland because the Polish Communist Party's commitment to its alliance with the Soviet Union was never in doubt. Hungary was different. The new prime minister, Imre Nagy, formed a coalition government and then announced plans to end the one-party system and withdraw Hungary from the Warsaw Pact. This represented a direct threat to Moscow's interests and on 4 November Soviet tanks moved into Budapest. By 7 November the revolution was over and over 30,000 Hungarians lost their lives; Nagy was arrested and executed. Khrushchev's military suppression of the Hungarian uprising showed just how far the Soviet Union was prepared to tolerate diversity within the communist bloc. The behaviour of Yugoslavia and Poland could be accommodated in the post-Stalin era because both countries remained rooted in the communist system, even if they took nationalist, non-Soviet forms. In Hungary the uprising was a popular, anti-communist revolt that aimed to overthrow a one-party dictatorship.

In the same week that the Soviet Union put down the Hungarian revolt Britain and France joined Israel in an attack on Egypt in response to Colonel Nasser's nationalisation of the Suez Canal. Only a year earlier Khrushchev had established the Soviet Union as a power in the Middle East for the first time when he made an arms deal with Nasser. Although the Anglo–French invasion was a military success, the refusal of the United States to support its allies, Soviet threats and condemnations from other countries soon led to the troops' withdrawal.

The year 1956 was a watershed in international politics. Both the Western and Soviet systems suffered deep shocks at their most vulnerable points. In the case of Britain and France the Suez crisis marked the end of their imperial power and left a power vacuum in the Middle East that would be filled by the United States and, to a lesser extent, by the Soviet Union. The Soviet Union's warning to Britain and France not to go further against Egypt marked its emergence as a power to be reckoned with in the Middle East. In the case of Eastern Europe, the

Soviet Union recovered its balance and was able to restore at least a surface unity to its empire.

## The era of nuclear confrontation: Berlin and Cuba, 1957–62

The half-decade from 1957 to 1962 has been called the 'nuclear epoch', a time when the danger of nuclear war was greater than ever before or since.[7] On 4 October 1957 the Soviet Union launched the first man-made satellite, called Sputnik, into orbit around the earth. It was a spectacular scientific achievement that alarmed the United States, not least because of its military implications. If the Soviets had a rocket capable of putting a satellite into orbit they could also produce a rocket with sufficient thrust to launch an inter-continental ballistic missile (ICBM) with a nuclear warhead against a target in the United States. At a stroke the Soviet Union seemed to have changed the East–West strategic balance.

Khrushchev took immediate diplomatic advantage of the Soviets' apparent lead in missile technology. He sought to detach West Germany and Britain from NATO, for example, by issuing crude threats about how they could be 'wiped from the face of the earth'.[8] Not surprisingly, one response in Britain to these open threats was the founding of the Campaign for Nuclear Disarmament (CND) in 1958. In fact, the so-called 'missile gap' in favour of the Soviet Union turned out to be a myth. By 1960 the Soviet Union had a total of only 4 ICBMs and 145 long-range bombers. The United States had over-whelming nuclear strategic superiority throughout the 1950s.

In fact Khrushchev could only have engaged in his nuclear diplomacy on the assumption that actual war was unlikely. He observed that the United States' behaviour towards the Geneva Summit, the Hungarian Revolution, the Suez Crisis and the Taiwan Straits showed an extreme reluctance to risk nuclear war. Domestically, Khrushchev's position was not secure and the economy was in trouble. He needed a foreign policy success against the United States. Indeed, his foreign policy adventures in the years 1958–62 were caused in part by the weakness, not the strength, of the Soviet Union in general and Khrushchev in particular.

Khrushchev sparked off the Berlin crisis in November 1958 when he issued an ultimatum to the Western powers demanding an end to their occupation of West Berlin and its transformation into a 'free city'. If the West did not sign a new treaty with Moscow by May 1959, the Soviet Union would sign a separate treaty with the German Democratic Republic (GDR). This would give the GDR control over access routes to West Berlin. The Soviet Foreign Minister, Andrei Gromyko, warned that any action taken against the GDR could start 'a big war in the crucible of which millions upon millions of people would perish'.[9] The West seemed to face a choice: withdraw from West Berlin or fight the Soviet Union.

The situation in Germany itself had changed fundamentally since 1955. West Germany had joined NATO and all immediate hope of German re-unification had vanished. Moscow accepted a divided Germany and now pressed for its corollary – Western recognition of East Germany. The West refused to recognise the East German regime because the latter had never held free elections. The West also held out the hope of a re-unified Germany in the future and therefore did not want to legitimise the *status quo*. But the Soviet Union wanted more than recognition of East Germany by the West. Moscow wanted to break the link between West Germany and the United States; this became almost an obsession with Khrushchev in the late 1950s.

Now that the Soviet Union had sufficient nuclear strength, Khrushchev acted to solve the Berlin problem. The contrast between East and West Germany was striking. West Germany had a booming economy in the 1950s, whereas East Germany's was stagnant. Berlin represented the one hole in the Iron Curtain. From 1949 to 1958 over 2.1 million East Germans (out of a population of 17 million in 1949) had escaped to West Germany. But in terms of military strength the Soviet Union had an overwhelming advantage: the West's garrison in Berlin totalled 11,000 men; they were surrounded by over half-a-million Eastern bloc troops outside the city.

The West refused to budge over Berlin and Khrushchev made his first retreat in March 1959 when he withdrew the ultimatum deadline of 27 May. Moscow realised as much as the West that it was unthinkable to use military force, which could quickly escalate into a full-scale nuclear war. A stalemate existed over Berlin for the next two years. During this time Khrushchev visited the United States, but, more important, he came under heavy criticism from China for pursuing a revisionist foreign policy. The schism between the Soviet Union and China, which opened in 1959, had a direct impact on Khrushchev's foreign policy (see Chapter 5). More than ever, he needed a diplomatic triumph over the West.

In the summer of 1961 Khrushchev believed the time was right to test the resolve of the new president. Kennedy had just suffered a set-back in the Bay of Pigs incident (April 1961), when a group of Cuban exiles, supported by the CIA, failed to overthrow the Castro regime in Cuba. A Berlin crisis was looming, with the arrival of over 1,000 East Germans a day into West Berlin in July, caused mainly by the fear that Khrushchev might cut off all access points to the city. The dramatic 'solution' to the problem came on 13 August 1961, when East Germany set up the Berlin Wall.[10]

The Wall solved the refugee problem at a stroke, but at the same time it became a symbol all over the world of repression in the Soviet sphere. Khrushchev withdrew his threat to make a separate peace treaty with East Germany and the Berlin crisis came to an end. He had failed to dislodge the West from Berlin and had come under fierce criticism from China for capitulating to the capitalist powers. Khrushchev still needed a foreign policy success. What began in Berlin in 1958 ended in Cuba in 1962.

## Cuba, 1962

The most dangerous nuclear crisis of the cold war took place over 13 days in October 1962. It originated in the summer of 1962 when Khrushchev placed strategic, intermediate-range offensive missiles on the island of Cuba, just 90 miles off the coast of Florida. It ended when he agreed to withdraw the missiles on 28 October.

In January 1959 the corrupt Batista regime in Cuba was overthrown by a rural guerrilla army led by Fidel Castro. Castro's relations with the United States worsened after he nationalised American-owned businesses in Cuba. After the abortive, CIA-inspired Bay of Pigs invasion in April 1961, Castro turned to Moscow for military protection. When an

American U-2 reconnaissance flight discovered Soviet missile installations in Cuba in October 1962, President Kennedy imposed a naval blockade to stop any further shipments of missiles to Cuba. Kennedy then called for the removal of all Soviet offensive missiles from Cuba, under threat of invasion within 24 hours. Following a complicated exchange of letters, the Soviet Union agreed to withdraw its missiles, in return for a United States promise not to invade Cuba.

There are many theories to explain Khrushchev's behaviour in the Cuban missile crisis.[11] The most plausible is that he hoped to redress at a stroke the nuclear imbalance between the Soviet and the West. At the time of the crisis the Soviet Union had only a handful of ICBMs, while the United States had 144 missiles positioned on Polaris submarines, as well as 294 ICBMs. By placing the cheaper, medium- and intermediate-range missiles on Cuba the Soviet Union could double its first-strike nuclear capacity at relatively little expense. In short, the missile deployment in Cuba could be seen as a 'quick fix' – not a substitute for a long-term build-up of ICBMs, but a stop-gap measure.

The Cuban missile crisis was Khrushchev's last foreign policy fling and it proved a disaster from which he never recovered. For Moscow and Washington it marked the end of a tense period of nuclear brinkmanship. Within a year the two superpowers made three important arms control agreements. In June 1963 a direct 'hot line' telephone link was set up between Washington and Moscow. In August 1963 a Nuclear Test Ban Treaty was signed by the United States, the Soviet Union and Great Britain. Finally, the missile crisis stimulated both superpowers to agree to the Treaty on the Non-Proliferation of Nuclear Weapons, which was signed in 1969.

# 4

# The United States and Indochina, 1945–75

The Vietnam War was the longest war in United States history. Though varying in intensity and focus it lasted from 1954 to 1975, cost $150 billion and involved 2,700,000 servicemen. The United States dropped 10 million tonnes of bombs on Vietnam – more than the entire amount dropped in World War Two. The North Vietnamese enemy lost over 900,000 people, compared to 58,000 American dead. Yet the United States still lost the war. Why?

Why did the United States make such a massive commitment to a small, backward country over 10,000 miles away? The decision to become involved in Vietnam was later described by a top American official, George Ball, as 'probably the greatest single error made by America in its history'.[1] For over twenty years the United States persisted in its objective of keeping South Vietnam free from communism. The United States did not drift 'blindly' into the war – every stage of deepening involvement was taken only after much calculation. Still, the United States lost the war and had to make a humiliating withdrawal from Vietnam in 1975.

The consequences of the Vietnam war were no less important than the causes. By the end of the war many people in the West saw the United States as a greater threat to the security of the world than the Soviet Union. The anti-war argument had won the debate: United States involvement in Vietnam had come to be seen as at best a blunder and at worst a crime.[2]

In the sections below we shall seek to answer three questions: why the United States went into Vietnam; why it stayed in Vietnam; why it withdrew from Vietnam.

## The roots of United States involvement in Indochina, 1945–61

In October 1945 France returned to take control of Indochina and was met by the Vietminh resistance movement, led by Ho Chi Minh, who had fought against the Japanese and now sought Vietnam's independence. France was able to gain control only over the southern part of Vietnam and therefore had to fight a drawn-out war against the Vietminh guerrilla forces from 1946 to 1954. Only weeks after the outbreak of the Korean War in 1950 Washington began to support the French in what was now seen as an anti-communist struggle.

The Eisenhower administration saw Ho Chi Minh as an instrument of international communism and claimed that the 'loss' of Indochina would have a disastrous effect on the rest of South-east Asia. The domino theory – later to be ridiculed by critics of the Vietnam War – was born. Yet, as we have seen in Chapter 3, Eisenhower refused either to commit troops or to use nuclear weapons in support of the French in Vietnam. In May 1954 the French got themselves trapped by the Vietminh forces at Dien Bien Phu and were forced to surrender, an event that marked the end of French colonial rule in Indochina.

At the Geneva Conference of 1954 Vietnam was partitioned along the 17th Parallel with country-wide elections to be held in 1956. The years 1955–9 tend to be ignored in histories of the Vietnam war because neither North Vietnam nor the South (and its ally, the United States) was engaged in hostilities. But there are good reasons for taking these years as the real starting point for an understanding of the United States' objectives in Vietnam, rather than Truman's decision to aid the French in 1950.

Secretary of State Dulles set out to achieve two aims in 1954: first, to create a treaty organisation similar to NATO in South-east Asia to provide for collective defence against the advance of communism in the area; and second, to establish a viable, national state in South Vietnam to resist the communist threat from the North. The first aim was met by bringing together seven nations to form the South-East Asia Treaty Organization (SEATO) in 1954. The second aim was met by installing Ngo Dinh Diem, a devout Catholic and Vietnamese nationalist, living in exile in the United States, to head the South Vietnam government in 1954.

Diem took over a country devastated by war and in political turmoil. Almost a million people had left the communist North to settle in the South, while just under 100,000 Vietminh troops and supporters had gone to the North. Diem refused to hold elections in 1956 because he feared losing to the communists, and he had no solution to the country's political problems other than repression. Washington even considered withdrawing its support from the Diem regime. The reason it did not can be gleaned from an extract from a speech made by Senator (later President) J.F. Kennedy on 'America's Stake in Vietnam' in 1956:

Vietnam represents the cornerstone of the free world in Southeast Asia, the keystone in the arch, the finger in the dyke. Burma, Thailand, India, Japan, the Philippines and obviously Laos and Cambodia, are among those whose security would be threatened if the red tide of Communism overflowed into Vietnam.[3]

The United States poured more than $1 billion in economic and military assistance into Vietnam between 1955 and 1961. This aid prevented the collapse of Diem's regime, but did little to improve the living conditions in rural villages, where more than 90 per cent of the population lived. The South Vietnamese army was trained by the United States to fight a conventional war, not a war of rural insurgency. But Vietnam was not Korea. In Vietnam the communist guerrilla forces from within the South, supported increasingly by the North, engaged in insurgency warfare against the Diem regime.

One of the great problems in understanding the Vietnam War lies in identifying the communist opposition to the Diem regime and the precise role played by the North (and its allies, China and the Soviet Union) in the insurrection in the South. North Vietnam first gave formal support to insurgents in the South in 1959. In 1960 these insurgents formed the National Liberation Front (NLF), with the aim of overthrowing Diem's government. The term 'Viet Cong', which means Vietnamese communist, was applied to the NLF by the Americans. The membership of the NLF was mainly communist and at this time came from the South, but they were henceforth increasingly supported from the North.

In 1960 Laos was seen as a more dangerous problem than Vietnam. The pro-American government there was overthrown by a so-called neutralist group in 1960. Meanwhile in South Vietnam, Ngo Dinh Diem had brought South Vietnam to despair and revolution by his negative, oppressive policies. Dulles' experiment in 'nation building' was not working. President Kennedy took office in January 1961, at a time when cold war tensions had reached a dangerous level.

## The politics of escalation under Presidents Kennedy and Johnson, 1961–8

President Kennedy gathered around him a team of young, energetic activists – 'the best and the brightest', in the phrase of David Halberstam – who believed that the lesson of appeasement at Munich in 1938 was applicable to the war in Vietnam.[4] They reasoned that just as China had stood behind North Korea, so China was supporting North Vietnam, and behind China stood the Soviet Union. Thus the war in Vietnam was seen as a variation on the pattern of totalitarian aggression that the West had failed to resist at Munich.

Kennedy and his advisers were highly critical of the Eisenhower administration's reliance on nuclear weapons and the doctrine of 'massive retaliation'. They opted for 'flexible response' (i.e. the use of conventional military forces) to combat the new, more subtle forms of communist aggression, as practised in Vietnam. It has often been argued that the United States got drawn into the war inadvertently, through the deceit of military men. This was not the case. Both Kennedy and Johnson consciously pursued a strategy of flexible response. It was their way of bringing control and stability into war in a nuclear age; ironically, it was a strategy that broke down because the other side did not play by the same rules.

Kennedy's involvement in Vietnam has to be understood in the context of international events at the time. In 1961 the new administration suffered setbacks in Cuba and Laos, and in August the Berlin Wall went up. The President began sending military advisers to train the South Vietnamese army to take the offensive against the Viet Cong in the so-called 'strategic hamlet' programme. The aim of the plan was attrition, which, in Neil Sheehan's words, 'would grind up the Viet Cong in the same way that General Patton had minced the Wehrmacht in Europe'.[5] The body count became the all-important test of success. Yet by 1963 it was clear that the strategy was not working, mainly because the Diem regime had alienated the population by its oppressive behaviour. On 1 November 1963 Diem was overthrown in a *coup* and assassinated. Three weeks later, Kennedy himself was assassinated. At the time of his death the United States had 16,000 'military advisers' in South Vietnam.

Vice-President Lyndon Johnson took over from Kennedy and then won the 1964 election on his claim that 'we seek no wider war' in Vietnam.[6] But already in August 1964 American destroyers were hit by North Vietnamese torpedo boats in the Gulf of Tonkin. Johnson responded by ordering retaliatory air strikes against North Vietnamese torpedo boat bases and oil storage dumps. More important, he used the occasion of the Tonkin incident to secure the passage through Congress, by an overwhelming vote of 48–2, of a resolution authorising the President to take 'all necessary measures' to repel armed attack. The significance of the Gulf of Tonkin Resolution was that it gave the President a blank cheque to conduct the war as he wished, without consulting Congress. In 1965 Johnson began a campaign of air strikes against North Vietnam in response to an attack on the United States army barracks in Pleiku. At the same time (March 1965) the first United States ground forces landed at Da Nang to protect the air base there. Johnson escalated the war without declaring an open war policy. He did this because he feared that a full discussion of the war in Congress might result in an even greater extension of the war.

Johnson's Vietnam policy rested on the unexamined assumption that the enemy could be beaten easily whenever Washington decided to apply its military might. Partly for this reason Johnson never worked out a strategy appropriate for fighting this kind of war. The United States intervened directly in the war in 1965 in order to prevent the collapse of South Vietnam; but it could not translate its military power to political advantage and establish a viable government in Saigon. Johnson wanted a limited war to avoid provoking the entry of the Soviet

Union and China. At the same time he wanted a quick victory in order to forestall unrest at home. These aims were inconsistent with one another. Once the war began to go badly for the United States in the years 1965–8 the failure of this strategy revealed itself.

Air power stood at the heart of United States military strategy. In spite of the evidence on the limited effectiveness of air power in the Second World War and the Korean War, it was widely believed that bombing could destroy an enemy's warmaking capacity and force him to make peace. By 1967 all the major targets in the North (supply depots, factories, etc.) had been destroyed and yet the bombing had had little effect on the North's capacity to fight the war. Bombing raids were described as 'trying to weed a garden with a bulldozer'.[7]

Meanwhile, the war on the ground escalated dramatically between 1965 and 1967. In late 1967 General Westmoreland requested over 540,000 troops to carry out 'search and destroy' missions. But in a war without front lines or clear territorial objectives it was almost impossible to gauge military success and therefore the 'body count' became the only criterion of progress. However, Hanoi could easily sustain 10:1 kill ratios against itself and still dictate the pace of the war by choosing when and where to engage the enemy.

The turning point of the war came in December 1968 when the Viet Cong launched the Tet Offensive against all the major urban areas of South Vietnam. The Tet Offensive was in fact a military failure, but it was a psychological success because it marked the beginning of Washington's effort to withdraw from the war. In March 1968 Johnson made a dramatic speech in which he announced a limitation of the bombing, an offer to discuss a peace settlement with Hanoi and his decision not to run for president again.

### Nixon: Vietnamisation and withdrawal, 1969–75

The new President, Richard Nixon, and his foreign policy adviser, Henry Kissinger, took office in January 1969. Nixon had promised the voters in his election campaign that 'we will end the war and win the peace'.[8] Both Nixon and Kissinger feared that a precipitate withdrawal from Vietnam would do great damage to America's credibility as a world leader. They were also confident against the odds that North Vietnam would agree to a political settlement if enough military force was applied.

Nixon was able to begin a phased withdrawal of American combat troops from Vietnam by pursuing a policy of Vietnamisation, which meant that South Vietnam took increased responsibility for the war. But when no breakthrough occurred in the peace negotiations Nixon launched a controversial bombing campaign against supply lines in Laos and Cambodia in 1970. A cease-fire agreement was finally reached between Washington and Hanoi in January 1973. Nixon claimed 'peace with honour', but it was bought at a high price. More American bombs were dropped on Indochina during the Nixon era than under Johnson's presidency.

The Vietnam War ended not with the Paris agreements of January 1973, but when North Vietnamese troops captured Hue, Da Nang and Saigon in April 1975. The policy of Vietnamisation had failed because the South Vietnam regime was corrupt and unable to mobilise mass support. The United States emerged from the war with a tarnished image abroad and more deeply divided at home than at any time since the civil war.

### The United States' misadventure in Vietnam: an interpretation

Even before the collapse of South Vietnam on 30 April 1975 the debate over Vietnam within the United States had concluded. For at least the last five years of the United States' involvement in Vietnam barely a voice was raised in defence of further participation in the war. The critics of the war had won the argument. Vietnam had become the symbol of a mistaken foreign policy, an example of what has been called 'the arrogance of power'. The more extreme critics saw United States involvement in Vietnam as an evil comparable to the evils committed by Nazi Germany. One such critic, the US writer Frances Fitzgerald, wrote that the effects of United States bombing were 'indistinguishable' from genocide. The anti-war critics had won all the political and moral arguments.

In fact it is not difficult to see how the United States got involved in Vietnam. The success of its containment policy in Europe in the later 1940s led it to think that the same policies would work in South-east Asia in the 1950s and 1960s. Korea was the link between the two. The United States defended South Korea in 1950 against what it saw as a worldwide communist conspiracy. Imbued with the idea that communism was mono-lithic, Washington's policy-makers failed to see that Vietnam was an independent communist state. Many of the Vietnamese communists were nationalists before they became communists, and at no time were they mere agents of either the Soviet Union or China. Therefore, the professed American war aim, 'to stop communism' in South Vietnam, revealed itself as an empty slogan. Since Vietnamese communism was not controlled by the Soviet Union or China, the fate of South Vietnam was not relevant to the containment of Soviet or Chinese communism.

Robert McNamara was the Secretary of Defense under Presidents Kennedy and Johnson and helped to lead the United States into Vietnam. Indeed, Vietnam was often called 'McNamara's war'. Thirty years later, in a book entitled *In Retrospect: The Tragedy and Lessons of Vietnam*, he wrote a candid inside account of the errors of judgement that landed the United States in an unwinnable war. McNamara cited two contradictory premises that governed policy in the Kennedy years and were never thoroughly examined. One was that the fall of South Vietnam to communism would threaten the security of the United States. The second was that only the South Vietnamese could defend their own country and therefore Washington should limit its support to providing military training and economic aid.[9]

McNamara admitted to seeing communism in Vietnam as related to guerrilla insurgent movements in Burma, Indonesia, Malaya and the Philippines in the 1950s. These conflicts were not seen as nationalist movements, but as part of a concerted communist drive for hegemony in Asia. In the 1940s in Europe, the United States recognised Yugoslavia under Tito as a communist nation independent of Moscow. In the 1960s the United States viewed Ho Chi Minh not as a South-east Asian Tito but as another Fidel Castro, operating within the Soviet/Chinese communist orbit.

Working on these assumptions the United States failed to see the political nature of the war in Vietnam. After the overthrow of Diem in 1963 Washington became more deeply enmeshed in South Vietnam and ignored the view held by Kennedy that only the South Vietnamese could defend their own country. Johnson escalated the war by bombing North Vietnam and landing combat troops in the South. But the war could not have been won by bombing the North, even if the bombing were effective. The reason for this is that the roots of the war lay in the South. The United States tried to fight the Viet Cong guerrilla forces in the South with counter-insurgency methods. But they faced a guerrilla army that was indistinguishable from the rest of the population and therefore was impossible to defeat without physically destroying the whole population. Further, the Viet Cong guerrillas were fanatics fighting for a social revolution and national survival and were willing to die rather than admit defeat.

American military leaders claimed that they could have won the war had they not had geographical constraints imposed on them for fear of a collision with China and the Soviet Union. That may have been true in a narrow military sense, but it failed to take into account the fact that the war had to be won in South Vietnam and, in the end, it had to be won by the South Vietnamese. If containment of China and the Soviet Union was Washington's paramount interest, then it made little sense to focus exclusively on the containment of communism in Vietnam. Vietnam was the traditional enemy of China and Vietnamese nationalism had served as a barrier to the expansion of China into South-east Asia for a millennium. By the early 1970s it was becoming clear to some policy-makers in Washington that America's preoccupation with winning a war in a small, backward peninsula of South-east Asia was distorting its primary foreign policy aim – the global containment of Soviet and Chinese communist power. During the Vietnam War China had taken over from the Soviet Union the position of number one communist enemy in the eyes of Washington. Yet, as we shall see in Chapter 5, before the Vietnam war had run its course, China and the United States would reach a historic rapprochement.

# 5

# China between the superpowers, 1949–80

## China as 'half a superpower'

China's foreign policy in the post-1949 period was in large part moulded by the country's experience of the past century. Mao Zedong wanted China to play a pivotal role in world affairs from 1949, but his view of China's place in the world rested on two doctrines that he had formulated in the 1920s and 1930s.[1]

The first was the theory of 'semi colonialism' in which Mao argued that China was actually in a stronger position as the object of many great powers' attention than if it had been the outright colony of only one power. When China found itself isolated internationally in the 1960s Mao reminded his colleagues that once again there were two dogs (the United States and the Soviet Union) tussling over the Chinese bone of meat and because both were in contention neither would get it.

The second doctrine was the 'theory of the intermediate zone'. Mao argued that the real cold war struggle was not taking place in Europe between the two superpowers, but in the vast 'intermediate zone' of Asia, Africa and Latin America, where the struggle was between revolutionary nationalism and imperialism. China was to play a leading role in supporting countries in the Third World in the 1950s and 1960s to achieve independence. This was Mao's way of denying the importance of the Soviet–American rivalry.

Mao's two doctrines derived from China's history of dependence on foreign powers. After 1949 Chinese diplomacy continued to be determined by, and responsive to, the policies of the two superpowers. Compared to the United States and the Soviet Union, China was weak. China has been convincingly described by John Gittings as 'half a superpower'. All the more remarkable, then, that it was able, in spite of its weakness, to retain its freedom of action in international affairs after 1949.

China was unique in being the only power to influence the strategic balance between the two superpowers. It shifted from a close alliance with the Soviet Union in the 1950s to a rapprochement with the United States in the 1970s. In the 1960s China challenged the international order by its support for revolutionary movements in the Third World. Although only a limited regional power, China was the only country to have fended off successfully invasion by either of the two superpowers.

## The Sino–American confrontation in the 1950s and 1960s

Taiwan lay at the heart of Sino–American antagonism. In 1949 the United States recognised and supported the Nationalist regime of Chiang Kai-shek in Taiwan, whose openly stated policy was the re-conquest of the mainland. In addition, the United States supported the anti-communist regimes on the Pacific rim, such as those in South Korea, Japan, the Philippines, Thailand and Indonesia, and kept the People's Republic of China excluded from the United Nations.

The Korean War was the catalyst that prompted the United States to turn Taiwan into a major military base and extend the policy of containment to the Pacific rim. In 1951 Washington signed a United Defense Assistance Agreement with Taiwan promising to provide the Nationalist government with 'military material for the defence of Taiwan against possible attack'.[2] Although it was stipulated that the aid could only be used for defensive purposes, the United States allowed the Nationalist forces to gain effective control of several groups of offshore islands.

The People's Republic of China's response to Washington's support for the Nationalist regime in Taiwan was to subject some of the offshore islands to heavy shelling in 1954 and 1958.

China and the United States never went to war over Taiwan, but Beijing remained committed to its objective of 'liberating' the island. The experience of the Korean War and Washington's continued support for Chiang Kai-shek's regime in Taiwan convinced the Beijing authorities that the United States sought to isolate and undermine the People's Republic. The United States for its part saw China as the new leader of world revolutionary communism and the main instigator of subversive activity in South-east Asia and the Third World. China was perceived as an 'international outlaw'. It resolutely opposed all Soviet–American attempts to regulate the nuclear arms race and thereby acquired a reputation for irresponsibility.

Still, China took great care to avoid a direct military confrontation with the United States. In the Vietnam War the Chinese gave moral and material support to the North, but made it clear that they themselves would not intervene unless the United States attacked China or invaded North Vietnam. In spite of its revolutionary rhetoric, China acted with caution. Indeed, by the later 1960s China began to move closer to the United States because it found itself increasingly threatened by its former ally, the Soviet Union.

### The Sino-Soviet alliance and split, 1950–69

Mao Zedong had little choice in 1949 other than to 'lean to one side' towards the Soviet Union. After all, the Soviet Union was the only other major communist power in the world in 1949. In February 1950 the Sino–Soviet Treaty of Friendship, Alliance and Mutual Assistance was signed. It included a 30-year military alliance directed against Japan or any of its allies and a low-interest Soviet loan to China of $300 million. Yet by the end of 1960 the alliance was dead, the Soviet Union had withdrawn all technical and economic advisers from China and Mao Zedong and Khrushchev were openly denouncing one another. The Sino–Soviet schism of 1960 had a profound effect on the international relations of the cold war.

China was dissatisfied with the aid it had received from the Soviet Union in the 1950s. But more important was the Soviet Union's refusal to provide China with a nuclear capability in 1958. Moscow was perhaps willing to install nuclear weapons in China, but only on condition that they remain under Soviet control. The conflict over nuclear weapons was highlighted by the Taiwan crisis of 1958, when the Soviet Union made it clear to China that under no condition should the crisis develop to a point where Moscow would have to invoke the nuclear deterrent. China reached the conclusion that it would have to develop its own nuclear deterrent. The Soviet Union was an industrialised state with its own nuclear weapons and recognised status as a superpower. China, by contrast, was a predominantly agricultural state with a limited military capacity. Further, it was in direct conflict with the United States over Taiwan and had revolutionary objectives in the Third World. When Khrushchev met Eisenhower in Washington in 1959 it looked to China as if the Soviet Union was making an accommodation with the arch-enemy of communism – the United States.

China's disenchantment with the Soviet Union can only be understood against the backdrop of the growing ideological rift between Moscow and Beijing in the late 1950s. The key year was 1956, for it was then that Khrushchev launched his famous denunciation of Stalin at the 20th Party Congress and later called for 'peaceful co-existence' with the United States. The Chinese were outraged that Khrushchev had made a major shift in communist orthodoxy without consulting them. Khrushchev claimed that in a nuclear age it was necessary to revise the Leninist doctrine of the inevitability of war and seek to achieve a peaceful co-existence with the capitalist adversary, the United States. The Chinese, as a dissatisfied power still wedded to change through revolution, bitterly attacked Khrushchev's 'revisionist' foreign policy as an abandonment of socialist principles.

In 1958 China embarked on a new economic policy, the Great Leap Forward, whose object was to harness the energy of the people by setting up huge rural communes and thereby to dispense with Soviet aid. China was staking a claim to ideological pre-eminence in the world socialist camp. The Soviet Union responded by abruptly withdrawing all its economic assistance to China in 1960. The Sino–Soviet dispute had become an open schism. In the 1960s Sino–Soviet relations reached breaking point under the strain of three unrelated crises: the Cuban missile crisis (1962); the Sino–Indian War (1962); and the Sino–Soviet border dispute (from 1964).[3]

The 'capitulation' of the Soviet Union to the United States in the Cuban missile crisis convinced the Chinese that Moscow would never again risk confrontation with its adversary. The Nuclear Test Ban Treaty, signed by Washington and Moscow in 1963, forbade nuclear testing in the atmosphere. China refused to sign. Instead it went on to explode its first atomic bomb, without Soviet assistance, in October 1964. Another source of conflict between China and the Soviet Union occurred during the border war between China and India in 1962. Moscow took a neutral stand in the conflict but fulfilled its promise to provide India with engines for its jet planes.

The most important source of antagonism between Beijing and Moscow was the border dispute between them that flared up in 1964 and almost led to war in 1969. The Soviet Union occupied more than one million square miles of territory that the Russian Tsarist regime had taken from China in the nineteenth century. China insisted that the border between the two countries be redrawn. Tension was very high in China's northwest province of Xinjiang, where border clashes frequently took place between the two communist powers.

China found itself in a particularly vulnerable position. The Soviet Union was able to amass a huge military presence (including nuclear weapons) in the border areas that China could not hope to match. Nevertheless, during the Cultural Revolution – a period of internal ideological and political turmoil from 1966 to 1969 – China went to extraordinary lengths to show hostility towards the Soviet Union. Chinese fears of the Soviet Union reached a peak in 1968 when the latter invaded Czechoslovakia. Moscow justified its action by the Brezhnev Doctrine, which proclaimed the right of the Soviet Union to intervene in any communist country that was thought to be deviating from the orthodox line. By this time there were frequent clashes between guards on each side of the Sino–Soviet border in the north-west. In March 1969 a contingent of Chinese soldiers attacked a Soviet patrol on Damansky Island (known to the Chinese as Chempao) in the Ussuri River. This incident was followed by a full-scale military clash between the two sides – the closest they ever came to engaging in an all-out war. As we shall see in the next section, the Soviet threat to China propelled it into a *rapprochement* with the United States in the 1970s.

Meanwhile, China adopted a position of aloofness between the two superpowers and took the lead in supporting wars of liberation in the 'intermediate zone', or Third World. China began to court the Third World at the first Afro–Asian conference held in Bandung, Indonesia in 1955. In practice the support that China gave to the cause of world revolution was largely rhetorical. The one area where China was to make a contribution to a 'people's war' was in Vietnam.

When the United States began to pour combat troops into Vietnam in 1965, China responded by sending an estimated 50,000 men, mainly engineering and construction teams. But what is significant is the different response of China to the presence of United States troops in Vietnam, compared to a similar set of circumstances in Korea in 1950, when China aligned itself with the Soviet Union. In the late 1960s China refused to turn to the Soviet Union; indeed, it continued to defy both of the great powers, even when the Vietnam War was at its height. Far from repairing its relations with Moscow, China moved closer to the United States in the late 1960s, in spite of the American presence in Vietnam.

### Triangular diplomacy: China, the Soviet Union and the United States in the 1970s

China made a radical shift in its foreign policy in the late 1960s, but the threat from the Soviet Union alone is not enough to explain it. Michael Yahuda has called the year 1968 'a major turning point in international politics' because in that year Mao Zedong recognised that the United States had made a retreat from escalating the war in Vietnam.[4] As we have seen in Chapter 4, President Johnson refused to escalate the war after the Tet Offensive in January 1968 and announced that he would not offer himself for re-election. Two events – the United States' retreat from escalation in Vietnam, coupled with the Soviet invasion of Czechoslovakia – were taken by Mao to mean that American imperialism was on the defensive and Soviet imperialism was entering an offensive phase. The main danger to China, therefore, would come from the Soviet Union, not the United States.

During the same time China's image in the world was changing. Between 1969 and 1972 thirty-two countries

47

recognised the People's Republic of China as the sole legitimate government of China. In 1971 China was admitted to the UN and gained a permanent seat on the Security Council. Within the United States there was also a radical change of attitude towards China. The Nixon administration was eager to withdraw troops from Vietnam, but did not want to upset the balance of power in Asia. By establishing a triangular relationship with China and the Soviet Union, the United States hoped to gain diplomatic leverage from the dispute between the two communist powers. In particular, the Nixon administration believed that a Sino–American *rapprochement* would put pressure on Moscow to be more responsive to a whole range of issues, such as disarmament, arms control and European security.

The rapprochement of China and the United States took three years (1969–71) to achieve. It was an intricate process that has been likened to a political version of a 'courtship ritual', largely because so much of the wooing had to be done in secret.[5] President Nixon's historic visit to China in February 1972 signalled perhaps the most dramatic shift in United States foreign policy since the end of the Second World War. The two countries agreed to maintain close diplomatic contact, though not yet formal diplomatic relations. Washington and Beijing renounced any ambition to seek hegemony in East Asia. Taiwan still remained a major barrier to the resumption of normal relations between the United States and China. But Washington agreed to a phased withdrawal of all United States forces and military installations from the island and China left the date open as to when the problem of Taiwan would be solved.

The emergence of China as an important third independent power upset the bipolar relationship between the United States and the Soviet Union and introduced a 'great power triangle' into the cold war.[6] Although weak economically and militarily, China from the late 1960s presented a major obstacle to Soviet political and strategic interests. The Soviet Union was now confronted with two hostile fronts instead of one. China's main aim in bringing Washington and Moscow into a triangular relationship was to reduce Soviet-American collusion and to contain Soviet expansionism by China itself threatening to collude with the United States. The Sino–Soviet split had a profound effect on the world communist movement because it exploded the myth of a monolithic proletarian internationalism.

The Sino–Soviet conflict, oddly enough, had a fiercer quality to it than the Soviet–American conflict. For one thing, the United States and the Soviet Union had no common border, whilst China and the Soviet Union shared the longest border in the world. The Soviet–United States conflict was only three decades old; the Russian–Chinese confrontation, by contrast, stemmed from the mid-nineteenth century, when Tsarist Russia expanded into the Far East and Central Asia. Perhaps even more important was the fact that the Sino–Soviet quarrel contained an ideological element, which gave it a special intensity.

The Sino–Soviet conflict could be likened to the antagonism between two rival churches, each claiming to represent the true doctrine.[7] Each side saw the other as a heretic. Mao's China accused the Soviet Union of 'revisionism', that is, of deviating from the true faith of socialism. The Soviet Union charged China with pursuing a dangerous, even irrational, policy of confrontation with the capitalist West in a nuclear age. Neither Moscow nor Beijing would abandon its claim to primacy within the communist camp. In the 1970s and 1980s triangular power politics was characterised by either Beijing 'playing the American card' or Washington 'playing the China card' against the Soviet Union.

# 6

# The rise and fall of détente
# in the 1970s

## Soviet–American rapprochement, 1967–72

By the late 1960s the Soviet Union was facing a number of problems, in both domestic and foreign policy, that made it seek a closer relationship with the United States.[1] First, the economy was stagnating. In the 1950s the gross national product (GNP) in the Soviet Union had grown by over 6 per cent; by the late 1960s it had fallen to under 4 per cent. One way to increase productivity without reforming the system was to import technology from and increase trade with the West. A second and more important reason that persuaded Moscow to move towards détente with the West was its growing rift with China. As we have seen in Chapter 5, the Sino–Soviet split of the early 1960s had almost culminated in a war in 1969. It was now a matter of crucial importance for Moscow to keep China isolated from the West by itself seeking a détente with the West.

The third factor that pushed the Soviet Union into a better relationship with the United States stemmed from the need to avoid a nuclear confrontation. Here the drive towards détente arose not from a problem but an achievement – by the late 1960s the Soviets had reached a rough strategic nuclear parity with the United States. By 1971, for example, the Soviet Union had surpassed the United States in intercontinental ballistic missiles (ICBMs) by 1,300 to 1,054. The United States still remained ahead in many categories of arms, but it no longer possessed the overwhelming nuclear superiority of the past. Paradoxically, this meant that genuine arms negotiations between the two superpowers were possible for the first time. Previous attempts at arms control had failed because they always tended to freeze Soviet forces into a position of permanent inferiority.

By the late 1960s the United States was also ready to pursue a policy of détente. President Nixon declared in his inaugural address in January 1969 that 'after a period of confrontation we are entering an era of negotiations'.[2] It seems surprising on the surface that Nixon should have made détente the centrepiece of his foreign policy. After all, he had built his domestic political career as a hard-line anti-communist. But his policy must be understood within the context of changes in the international system.

The main problem facing the Nixon administration was how to end the Vietnam War and at the same time retain the United States' global role and continue to compete with the Soviet Union when the domestic consensus in favour of containment had broken down. Nixon's national security adviser, Henry Kissinger, called for a 'philosophical deepening' of American foreign policy.[3] By this he meant adjusting to the changed international order. The Kennedy and Johnson administrations, Kissinger argued, had focused too much on victory in one rather isolated area – Vietnam – at the expense of the global balance of power. The world was shifting from a bipolar balance of power between Washington and Moscow to a multipolar balance shared among five great economic and strategic centres – the United States, the Soviet Union, Western Europe, Japan and China.

The Nixon–Kissinger approach meant downplaying the role of ideology in foreign policy and recognising that military strength was not always decisive in world affairs. But, like George Kennan in the 1940s, Kissinger sought to influence the Soviet Union. Détente for America did not represent the end of the policy of containment; rather, it was, in the words of J.L. Gaddis, 'a means of updating and re-invigorating containment'.[4] It would be a mistake to assume that Moscow and Washington understood détente in the same way. As we shall see below, the United States saw détente as a means of disciplining Soviet power; the Soviet Union saw détente as providing a golden opportunity to extend its power.

## The high noon of détente, 1972–4: SALT I and détente in Europe

Détente reached its peak between the years 1972 and 1974 in a series of four summit meetings held between Moscow and Washington. At the core of the process lay the issue of arms control. Nixon and Kissinger brought a radical change in Washington's nuclear arms policy by insisting that sufficiency rather than superiority was enough. The Soviet Union had developed its strategic offensive forces in the 1960s and both sides were now worried about the costs of the arms race and the fact that either side might take a decisive lead in a particular area.

The Strategic Arms Limitation Talks (SALT), which began in 1969, were about arms control, not disarmament. In an age when the two superpowers could destroy each other completely with their nuclear weapons, both relied on a strategy of deterrence. Arms control was a way of safeguarding against threats to the stability of deterrence that had come about through developments in weaponry.

Computerised guidance systems, when linked to an intercontinental ballistic missile (ICBM) with high-yield warheads, could destroy an opponent's land-based ICBMs. The anti-ballistic missile (ABM) was a defensive weapon that had the potential to protect a city from attack and therefore upset the old doctrine of Mutual Assured Destruction (MAD), which was the basis of deterrence in the 1950s and 1960s. Finally, the development of multiple independently targeted re-entry vehicles (MIRVs) threatened to upset the strategic balance. One missile with a MIRV warhead on it could deliver over a dozen nuclear weapons to different targets.

The SALT I negotiations ended in 1972 having failed to reach a comprehensive agreement limiting strategic weapons. Instead, two lesser agreements were reached. First, there was an interim agreement fixing a five-year freeze on offensive strategic delivery vehicles (ICBMs were fixed at 1,054 for the United States and 1,618 for the Soviet Union; SLBMs at 656 for the United States and 740 for the Soviet Union; and long-range bombers at 455 for the United States and 140 for the Soviet Union). Second, a treaty was signed limiting each side to two ABM sites of no more than 100 missile launchers.

SALT I was criticised for not imposing sufficiently severe limitations on the United States and the Soviet Union. The ABM treaty, for example, limited each side to two ABM sites of no more than 100 missile launchers each. One site could protect the country's capital (Moscow or Washington) and the other could protect a major ICBM site. But, as it turned out, neither side intended to build an ABM system to the extent permitted by SALT I. Further, SALT has been called a 'crucial failure' because it did not include the development of MIRVs, which first the United States and then the Soviet Union continued to deploy.[5] Still, the very fact that Moscow and Washington had reached an arms agreement was itself an achievement. SALT I began a process of institutionalised arms control, confirmed the Soviet Union's parity with the United States and reduced tension between the two nuclear powers.

### Détente in Europe

Détente in Europe was linked to the superpower détente but it had different origins – the main impulse came from West Germany not the United States. In October 1969 the Social Democrats, in coalition with the Free Democrats, won control of the Bundestag for the first time and Willy Brandt became the new Chancellor. This represented a leftward shift in West German politics and a break from the rigid anti-communist policies of the outgoing Christian Democratic Party. Brandt's Eastern Policy, or *Ostpolitik*, sought to break down the barriers between the two German states and in general promote more human and economic contact between Eastern and Western Europe. Brandt believed that the Hallstein Doctrine – which stated that any country recognising East Germany would not be recognised by West Germany – was having the effect of isolating not East Germany but West Germany itself. For the Soviet Union the main objective of European détente was to win Western acceptance of the division of Germany and the territorial *status quo* in Eastern Europe.

In August 1970 the Soviet Union and the Federal Republic of Germany signed the Moscow Treaty, which was the closest thing to a peace treaty ending the Second World War. It must be remembered that no formal peace treaty had been signed in 1945 ending the war between Germany and the Allies. By this treaty West Germany confirmed the division of the German nation into two states and officially accepted the loss of pre-war German lands in the east to Poland and the Soviet Union. The Moscow Treaty was a triumph for Brezhnev because it won Western acceptance for the Soviet position in Germany and opened an era of détente in Europe.

The problem of Berlin was settled in the Final Quadripartite Protocol (1972), in which Moscow conceded that the Federal Republic could maintain and develop its special ties with West Berlin. It was a victory for Willy Brandt's *Ostpolitik*. The Soviet Union accepted the *status quo* in Berlin. Never again would it demand that West Berlin be an independent city or threaten to hand over its access routes to the East Germans. In December 1972 the Federal Republic and the German Democratic Republic signed the Basic Treaty, which accepted the *de facto* existence of two German states on German soil, although West Germany still declined to accord East Germany full diplomatic recognition.

Willy Brandt's *Ostpolitik* did much to reduce tension in the heart of Europe. But the Soviet Union was eager to go beyond the German problem and seek Western recognition of the legitimacy of the countries of Eastern Europe and acceptance of the *status quo* in the region. What emerged from the Conference on Security and Co-operation held at Helsinki was not a peace treaty, but a declaration of intent, known as the Final Act. The most controversial part of the Final Act was the so-called 'Basket 3', which pledged the signatories to respect human rights.

Critics of the Helsinki Conference found it difficult to reconcile many provisions of the Final Act with the Soviet invasion of Czechoslovakia in 1968, the Brezhnev Doctrine justifying that invasion, and the dismal record on human rights in the Eastern bloc countries. The West seemed to gain nothing more than vague promises of good behaviour from the Soviet Union. When the Eastern bloc governments made no real improvements in their handling of human rights issues, disillusionment with détente set in rapidly in the West, as we shall see in the next section.

# The decline of détente

Détente was riddled with more contradictions than either Washington or Moscow was prepared to admit. Moscow wanted co-operation from the West over arms control, trade and central Europe but was not willing to accept the *status quo* in other areas. The Soviet Union was intent on expanding its influence in the Third World. This is where détente was put to the test.

Its first real challenge came in the Middle East War of October 1973, when Syria and Egypt attacked Israel during the Yom Kippur holiday. As the Soviet Union had withdrawn its military personnel from Egypt before the invasion, it was suspected that it had had previous knowledge of the invasion. Only months earlier Nixon and Brezhnev had signed an agreement to inform one another of any conflict that might threaten world peace. It is true that the crisis did not develop into a war between the two superpowers, but belief in détente was shaken, especially in the United States.

The Soviet Union's activist policy in Africa in the 1970s was a major reason for the decline of détente. In 1975 Portugal's largest and richest colony, Angola, was torn by civil war in the run-up to independence. The Popular Movement for the Liberation of Angola (MPLA) was able to gain victory by massive Soviet military aid (in the form of tanks, planes and rocket-launchers) and the arrival of 12,000 Cuban combat troops. It was the first time that communist military forces had intervened on such a massive scale in Africa. The reaction in the United States was extreme. President Ford, who had succeeded Nixon in August 1974, banned the word 'détente' from his political vocabulary.

The Soviet Union and Cuba intervened again in Africa in 1977 when they supported Ethiopia in expelling Somalia from the Ogaden region. The sheer scale of the Soviet involvement alarmed Washington and, combined with Soviet action else-where, made it seem as though Moscow was engaged in a geopolitical offensive on a broad front. Soviet arms, for ex-ample, had helped North Vietnam to victory over the South in 1975 and North Yemen's victory over South Yemen in 1979 was also made possible by Soviet arms. President Carter's security adviser, Zbigniew Brzezinski, referred to the Soviet geopolitical offensive as 'the arc of crisis', but it is unclear whether Moscow acted from a grand design, or out of an opportunistic response to unconnected regional disputes. In any case, it took full advantage of the United States' post-Vietnam aversion to foreign adventures.

The Soviet and Cuban involvement in the Horn of Africa fuelled the arguments of the domestic critics of President Carter's foreign policy, who accused him of failing to compete more vigorously with the Soviet Union. The Southern Democrat Jimmy Carter had come to power in 1977 on a wave of anti-military, anti-Washington opinion, following the Vietnam War and the Watergate affair. But Carter's liberalism was only a brief interregnum in a longer-term shift in United States politics towards the right. The backlash in favour of a return to more traditional cold war policies was already in motion in the late 1970s. Détente was also a casualty of this trend.

Another strand in the unravelling thread of détente was the SALT II negotiations. Agreement was finally reached in 1979 to set a ceiling of 2,400 missile launchers (ICBMs and SLBMs) and heavy bombers for each side. A maximum was also set for the number of launchers that could be fitted with MIRVs. Although neither side gained a decisive advantage from SALT II, there was a mounting fear in the United States that the Soviet Union was building up a strategic superiority, based mainly on the weight and numbers of its ICBMs. When a Soviet combat brigade was discovered in Cuba in 1979 the United States Senate refused to ratify SALT II, and that spelled the end of arms control and détente.

The final death blow to détente came with the Soviet Union's invasion of Afghanistan in December 1979. President Carter described the Soviet invasion, with some exaggeration, as 'the greatest threat to world peace since World War Two'.[6] Whether the Soviet Union acted out of a clear-cut strategic plan to expand its influence into the Persian Gulf region or merely responded to a local situation is not entirely clear. What mattered was the effect of the invasion.

The Soviet Union had a strong interest in preventing an anti-communist Islamic republic from existing on its borders. For this reason 80,000 Soviet troops were sent to Afghanistan to preserve in power the government of Babrak Karmal, which had just been installed by Moscow. The scale of the invasion shocked the United States and provoked the Carter administration to go back to the traditional strategy of containment. The return to cold war rhetoric and policies came not with the Republican administration of Ronald Reagan in 1981, but with the Carter administration during his last year in office.

## Détente – a failure?

Washington and Moscow had different expectations from détente. For the United States, Henry Kissinger, Nixon's influential national security adviser and later Secretary of State, articulated the view that Soviet–American competition should be regulated and both powers encouraged to co-operate in arms development and the Third World. Kissinger's vision of détente reflected the changed position of the United States in a world where it no longer had undisputed military superiority.

The Soviet Union wanted to control the arms race, increase trade links with the West and win recognition of its status as an equal superpower. After suffering from decades of strategic inferiority the Soviet Union had achieved nuclear parity and now wished to exercise the power that reflected its new position. As we have seen, this meant expanding its influence in the Third World, a process that brought détente to an end.

When Ronald Reagan became president in January 1981 détente was written off as a failure and Moscow was blamed for its demise. But was it a failure? Some historians have taken a more sympathetic view of détente than American politicians did at the time. J.L. Gaddis, for example, has argued that the charge of failure is based on a misunderstanding of what détente was about in the first place.[7] It was not intended to end the arms race, eliminate Soviet–American rivalry in the Third World, or provide the instrument of reform within the Soviet Union, even if popular rhetoric often made such claims for it. Its purpose was rather to work with the Soviet Union in order to prevent differences between the two superpowers from exploding into dangerous crises.

At a more modest level détente did score some achievements. The SALT I agreements limited the development of certain strategic weapons. A chronic trouble spot in the cold war – Berlin – was eliminated by détente in Europe. Soviet power in the Middle East declined dramatically and Moscow became more dependent economically on the West than ever before.

Perhaps most important of all, détente put an end to Washington's fixation with what Kissinger called 'a small peninsula on a major continent' – Vietnam – and brought its attention back to more central global concerns.

Still, from Washington's point of view, détente failed to achieve its aims in three main areas: linkage; the military balance; and human rights. The objective of linkage was to try to change Soviet behaviour through a system of positive and negative reinforcements. It failed partly because the United States did not have a clear vision of what it wanted from the Soviet Union. The main reason for this was the divided authority between the presidency and Congress: Congress, often dominated by the rival political party, would reject agreements made by the President. For example, Senator Jackson ruined the Soviet–American trade agreement of 1972 by demanding an increase in Jewish emigration from the Soviet Union before credits and most-favoured nation status would be granted. The Soviet Union, however, was given to believe by the Nixon administration that the trade agreement was concluded as a reward for its co-operation over Berlin, SALT, the Middle East and Vietnam.

Détente failed to achieve a real military balance. It was never the aim of Nixon and Kissinger to allow the Soviets to gain an advantage in certain strategic weapons. Quite the reverse, the Nixon administration intended to pursue a military build-up in areas not restricted by the SALT I agreement – the B1 bomber, the Trident submarine and the MX cruise missile. But, in the aftermath of the Vietnam War, Congress imposed deep cuts on all military expenditures and, therefore, the United States fell behind the Soviet Union in certain categories of strategic weapons. Détente took the blame for this, but the situation was really caused by the anti-military sentiment in Congress.

The third area of failure was that of human rights. One of the most persistent criticisms made of détente was that it ignored the moral dimension of foreign policy. Kissinger and Nixon were accused in their foreign policy of placing stability and order above justice and morality. It is true that both men relied on secrecy, for instance, in negotiations with China and in talks over arms control. This meant that they failed to convince Congress and the public of the merits of their strategy. But they also made the mistake of claiming too much for détente. The best example of this was the Helsinki agreement on human rights in 1975, which raised expectations in the West about improved behaviour in this field in the Soviet bloc that simply could not be fulfilled.

# 7

# Reagan, Gorbachev and the end of the cold war, 1981–91

## The Reagan presidency and the 'second' cold war, 1981–5

The election of Ronald Reagan in 1980 represented a sea change in US politics and came at a time when Soviet–American relations were at their lowest ebb for twenty years. Reagan denounced America's foreign policy of the 1970s in uncompromising terms. His critique of détente and arms control centred around three main propositions. First, it was impossible for Washington to have a stable relationship with a 'totalitarian' country. Second, under the guise of arms control (SALT I and II), the Soviet Union had actually gained a position of military superiority over the West. Third, the United States' loss of military pre-eminence was not inevitable; on the contrary, it was possible to restore its military 'margin of safety'.[1]

Reagan was a conviction politician whose instincts were to confront the Soviet Union in an ideological way. In 1983 he denounced the Soviet Union as an 'evil empire'. Yet this confrontational attitude did not translate itself into a confrontational policy. George Schultz, who was appointed Secretary of State in 1982, called for arms control with Moscow and Reagan himself said, 'we are ready for constructive negotiations with the Soviet Union', only one year after the 'evil empire' speech.[2] The Soviet Union, under its new leader, Yuri Andropov, warned that the two countries were on a collision course if the United States continued to pursue a policy of military superiority.

The Reagan administration was determined to resume arms control negotiations only when it had achieved a position of military strength. To this end the administration launched a five-year programme, costing $180 billion, to modernise the country's strategic forces. But the growth of anti-nuclear movements in Europe and the 'freeze' movement in the United States put pressure on Washington to return to the bargaining table.

The first problem to deal with was that of intermediate-range nuclear weapons in Europe. Since 1971 the Soviet Union had been deploying the SS-20 missile, a new, more accurate intermediate-range nuclear weapon facing Western Europe. NATO had no comparable missile and therefore, under pressure from Western European leaders, Washington had agreed to the famous 'twin-track' decision in 1979: first, to deploy Pershing II ballistic missiles in West Germany and ground-launched cruise missiles in several other European countries, including the UK; second, to propose to the Soviet Union that NATO would not deploy its weapons in return for the withdrawal of all SS-20s from European soil. Reagan put forward the 'zero option' at the INF talks in 1981, but the Soviet Union rejected it. When NATO began deploying Pershing and cruise missiles in November 1983 Moscow broke off talks altogether.

The year 1983 was the worst in Soviet–American relations since the Cuban missile crisis. The START (Strategic Arms Reduction Talks) negotiations, which had opened in 1982 to discuss strategic nuclear forces, broke down at the same time as the INF talks. Earlier, in March 1983, Reagan announced his Strategic Defense Initiative (SDI), which would provide a protective shield of laser and particle beam weapons in space against ballistic missiles. This 'Star Wars' speech was not just another proposal to solve the problem of the United States' vulnerability to incoming missiles. It shifted the whole strategic landscape by rendering offensive weapons impotent. Reagan had always been uncomfortable with the doctrine of mutual assured destruction (MAD), and 'Star Wars' provided him with what Lawrence Freedman has called the 'Great Escape from the nuclear dilemma'.[3] Most scientists claimed that it was impossible in practice to build a totally effective defensive shield in space and, as we shall see, the idea was abandoned by Reagan's successor, George Bush. But Moscow took SDI seriously in the 1980s as a dangerous dream by a president intent on seeking an alternative to arms control. The Soviet Union took SDI seriously because, if implemented, it would have made the United States immune to a Soviet attack and thereby upset the equilibrium between the two superpowers, based on mutual assured destruction.

Reagan's attacks on détente and arms control and his insistence on building a strong nuclear defence caused great tension with the United States' Western European allies. The deployment of Pershing and cruise missiles in 1983, far from reassuring the Europeans, had the opposite effect. Then Reagan's unilateral announcement of SDI led many Europeans to see the greatest threat to war coming not from Soviet behaviour but from the arms race itself and the United States' assertive behaviour. Western Europe was still committed to the pursuit of its own separate détente with the Soviet Union. In Poland the anti-communist trade union, Solidarity, arose in 1980 and was put down when General Jaruzelski's regime imposed martial law in 1981. Relations between the United States and Europe were further strained when Washington imposed economic sanctions on both Poland and the Soviet Union.

President Reagan came to office in 1981 convinced, in his own words, that 'the Soviet Union underlies all the unrest that is going on' in the world.[4] The administration chose to defend the right-wing Central American government of El Salvador against militant, left-wing guerrilla forces. Reagan's ambassador to the UN, Jeanne Kirkpatrick, made the famous distinction between 'authoritarian' dictatorships, which were friendly to the United States and could evolve into democracies, and left-wing 'totalitarian' dictatorships, which could not. Reagan hoped to stop the supply of arms from nearby Nicaragua to the guerrillas in El Salvador. When Congress refused to provide support for the counter-revolutionary forces (the 'Contras') in Nicaragua, Reagan bypassed this decision and continued to support the 'freedom fighters' with secret funds.

## Gorbachev and Reagan, 1985–9

During Reagan's first administration, the Soviet Union was going through a transitional phase caused by the deaths of three leaders in three years. Leonid Brezhnev died in November 1982, Yuri Andropov in February 1984 and Konstantin Chernenko in March 1985. The Kremlin in these years has been described as 'doubling as a geriatric ward and funeral parlour'.[5] Worse, the country was in the throes of a political crisis caused by the increasing sclerosis of the Soviet economy. The growth rate had been declining for two decades, from over 5 per cent in the 1960s to 2 per cent in the early 1980s. More revealing was the backwardness of the Soviet Union in key technologies – micro-electronics and computers – where the gap between the Soviet Union and the West was growing wider.

The Soviet Union was a curious superpower: militarily, it was the equal of the United States, but in economic terms it lagged far behind its rival.[6] It had a low *per capita* gross national product, its products were of poor quality and a large pro-portion of its population was engaged in agriculture, which suffered repeated harvest failures. The economy, with its high percentage of raw material exports, resembled more that of a developing country of the Third World than a capitalist eco-nomy of Western Europe or the United States. By the early 1980s the 'correlation of forces' (a Marxist term used to describe the strength of competing countries) was moving against the Soviet Union.

Within hours of the death of Chernenko on 11 March 1985, the Plenum of the Central Committee elected Mikhail Gorba-chev as General Secretary of the Party. The 54-year-old Gorba-chev belonged to a new generation that had no memories of Stalin's terror and the Second World War.[7] He was therefore able to formulate a revolutionary domestic and foreign policy. The consequences of these policies, though not the intentions, would lead to the dismantling of the Soviet empire in Eastern Europe, the end of the cold war and the break-up of the Soviet Union itself.

Under Gorbachev's leadership two new Russian words entered the language of politics: *perestroika*, meaning restructuring, and *glasnost*, meaning openness. The concept of *glasnost* represented a break from the old Bolshevik notion of a vanguard party, in possession of the 'correct' line, ruling over the backward mass of the people. But as we shall see, *glasnost* was a double-edged sword that could be used by groups opposed to the unchallenged rule of the Communist Party. Openness could work in two ways:

it could allow the flow of new ideas from outside the party to instigate political debate, but at the same time it could undermine the authority of the Communist Party. What began as a reform would end in a revolution. Meanwhile, Gorbachev called for new thinking in international affairs. He said there could be 'no winners' in a nuclear war and declared the world to be interdependent, likening all its people 'to climbers roped together on the mountainside'.[8]

The accession of Gorbachev to power in March 1985 marked the beginning of the end of the cold war – indeed, he set out deliberately to end it. Arms control lay at the heart of the search for a political accommodation with the United States. Gorbachev and Reagan met in four summit meetings between 1985 and 1988 and transformed the chilly relationship between their two countries into one of trust and conciliation by the end of the decade.

At their first summit meeting in Geneva in November 1985 no concrete results were achieved, but the two leaders agreed in their communiqué that 'a nuclear war cannot be won and must not be fought'.[9] This statement represented a significant shift in Soviet thinking and pointed to the possibility that the Soviet Union might consider reducing its ICBM force. But Soviet opposition to SDI proved to be the main stumbling block to any practical agreement in arms control.

The second summit meeting between Reagan and Gorbachev was held at a reputedly haunted house in Reykjavik, Iceland, in October 1986. It was to prove the most bizarre meeting in the history of nuclear diplomacy. Contrary to each country's expectations, the agenda at Reykjavik turned out to be not arms control, or even arms reduction, but that most implausible theme of the nuclear age – complete disarmament. In the final session Reagan called for the elimination of all ballistic missiles within ten years. Gorbachev insisted that United States research on SDI must be confined to the 'laboratory'. Reagan would make no concessions over SDI and the summit ended in failure.

The dream of a nuclear-free world entertained by Reagan and Gorbachev remained just that, a dream. Behind the collapse of the main talks, however, the foundations were laid for later agreements at a lower level in three areas: the elimination of American and Soviet land-based intermediate-range missiles; a major reduction of strategic offensive weapons; and a joint pledge not to withdraw from the ABM Treaty or to deploy SDI for an agreed period of time.

The Reykjavik meeting failed because agreement on reduction in strategic and medium-range weapons hinged on an agreement over space weapons. It was an all-or-nothing package. At the third summit meeting in Washington in December 1987 Gorbachev untied the package and offered an entirely separate proposal to eliminate one class of nuclear weapons – land-based missiles of intermediate and shorter range.[10]

The Intermediate-Range Nuclear Force Treaty (INF Treaty) was an important first step in reducing the nuclear arsenals of the two powers. Agreement was also reached on a comprehensive process of verification for the first time in the history of arms control. State inspections were authorised to acquire data and witness the destruction of missiles. The INF Treaty was a milestone in nuclear arms negotiations because it showed that it was possible not merely to restrain but to reverse the arms race.

The fourth summit took place in Moscow in May 1988 and failed to reach an agreement on how to cut the strategic nuclear weapons of each power. Again, the stumbling block was failure to agree about SDI. Yet the inconclusive nature of the fourth summit did little to check the momentum of arms reduction negotiations. More important, Gorbachev almost single-handedly wiped out the Americans' view of the Soviet Union as the 'evil empire'.

In spite of Gorbachev's brilliant public relations exercise on behalf of his country, it is probably accurate to describe the substance of his foreign policy as a 'diplomacy of decline'.[11] The arms control agreements made with Washington demanded more cuts on the Soviet side than the United States. The Soviet Union lost the propaganda campaign against the deployment of NATO cruise and Pershing missiles. Moscow agreed to a phased withdrawal of Soviet troops from Afghanistan in April 1988, without any guarantee that their choice of leader in Kabul would survive. In Eastern Europe the political and economic reforms gained such momentum that the entire Soviet empire collapsed there in 1989. Owing to a combination of economic and political factors, communism as a world movement had lost its authority and legitimacy by the end of the 1980s. The 'success' of Gorbachev's foreign policy is all the more remarkable against the backdrop of an empire in terminal decline.

Reagan's foreign policy during his presidency from 1981–9 has baffled commentators.[12] On the one hand, his administration has been strongly criticised for its 'aggressive' foreign policy in Central America and for its belief in the feasibility of a modern nuclear missile shield, SDI. In 1986 it was revealed that the administration was secretly selling arms to Iran to provide aid for the anti-communist Contra rebels in Nicaragua. The so-called Iran–Contra affair did much damage to Reagan's presidency. On the other hand, Reagan deserves credit for changing the whole nature of the nuclear debate with the Soviet Union. Under Reagan the sterile process of arms limitations was transformed into creative negotiations about arms reductions. Reagan was the key figure in starting the new cold war of the early 1980s; he was also the moving force in bringing about a genuine accommodation with the Soviet Union in the later 1980s.

## 1989: the year of revolution in Eastern Europe

This was a miraculous year in the history of post-war Europe. In the space of a few short months all the communist regimes in Eastern Europe within the Soviet sphere of influence had crumbled and disappeared. Timothy Garton Ash, a British journalist, arrived in the middle of the Czech revolution on 23 November and declared to the future president, Vaclav Havel: 'In Poland it took ten years, in Hungary ten months, in East Germany ten weeks! Perhaps in Czechoslovakia it will take ten days'.[13]

Each country in Eastern Europe had its own reasons for overthrowing its communist government, but three themes are common to all the countries involved.[14] First, the role played by the Soviet leader, Mikhail Gorbachev. He publicly dissociated himself from the Brezhnev Doctrine, which had stated that the Soviet Union had the right to intervene militarily in a socialist country in order to keep it within the socialist fold. The fact that the Soviet Union would not automatically support with troops an Eastern European communist regime threatened by revolution now made a revolution possible. A second reason for the revolutions in 1989 is a simple one – communism never enjoyed mass popular support. In every East European satellite state communism had been imposed from without and this had given rise to violent resistance movements. There had been uprisings in East Germany in 1953, in Hungary in 1956, in Czecho-slovakia in 1968 and in Poland in 1980. No one could predict that 1989 would be a year of successful revolutions, but the prospect of revolution was always present in these authoritarian countries. A third reason for the events of 1989 was the slow economic growth of the East European countries in the previous decade. At a time when Western Europe was confidently expanding, Eastern Europe was stagnating with slow growth, high foreign debts and a low *per capita* gross domestic product.

During Brezhnev's period of office (1965–82) Soviet influence was at its most negative, which meant that reform from within the communist regimes of Eastern Europe was ruled out. The beginnings of the great groundswell against communism took place in Poland with the birth of the trade union movement Solidarity, in the summer of 1980. Led by Lech Walesa, an electrician at the Lenin Shipyard in Gdansk, Solidarity broadened its demands to include genuinely independent unions, the end of press censorship and the release of political dissidents. Solidarity was driven underground when martial law was imposed in 1981, but it continued to grow in the 1980s. By 1988 the Polish economy was in desperate shape and this put pressure on the Government to legalise Solidarity and promise to hold elections in the following year. The elections of June 1989 resulted in the elimination of the entire communist leadership, whilst Solidarity won 99 out of 100 seats in the Senate. In December the parliament formally removed the Party's leading role in Government and restored the pre-war name, the Republic of Poland, to the nation. The dead hand of communism was finally severed from the Polish body.

In Hungary, unlike Poland, the impetus for reform came from within the party. Janos Kadar, who had led the Hungarian Communist Party since 1956, was removed by the party and Imre Nagy, the executed leader of the 1956 revolution, was reburied in what mounted to a ceremony of rehabilitation. In October 1989 the new Hungarian Republic was declared and free elections were held in March 1990.

East Germany (the German Democratic Republic) was different from all the other countries in Eastern Europe. It was not so much a nation as a state built on an ideological concept – socialism. The only reason for its existence was the maintenance of socialism: the moment socialism lost its credibility, East

67

Germany collapsed as a state. Unlike Poland and Hungary, the East German government fell not after a period of reform, but because it refused to reform. Behind the protection of the Berlin Wall since 1961 East Germany revived economically in the 1960s, but by the 1980s its economy was stagnating. When Hungary opened its barbed wire border with Austria in May 1989 it was no longer possible to prevent the flood of refugees leaving East Germany. Huge demonstrations by the people against the Government culminated in the collapse of the Berlin Wall on 9 November 1989, which doomed the communist regime.

The revolution in Czechoslovakia in 1989 took just ten days to complete, from 17 November to 27 November. The reform movement in Czechoslovakia was the work of political amateurs, led by the playwright Vaclav Havel, who had spent many years in prison for supporting political dissidents. Demonstrations in Prague in November calling for the resignation of the Communist Party led to the toppling of the regime. On 30 December 1989 Havel was elected President. The communist regime under Topol Zhivkov in Bulgaria was also overthrown in November 1989. Romania was the last East European country to have a revolution. The overthrow of President Ceauşescu on 25 December 1989 took place only after a violent battle between crowds of people and the security guards in the centre of Bucharest.

A remarkable feature of all the revolutions, with the exception of Romania, is that they were peaceful. Unlike the revolutions in Europe of 1848, to which they have been compared, there was no counter-revolution in 1989. The so-called 'Peoples' Democracies' of Eastern Europe were regimes imposed on the people from the outside and buttressed by the might of the Soviet Union. When Gorbachev made clear that the Soviet Union would no longer support them, they collapsed. What, then, was the dominating idea behind the revolutions of 1989? Ralf Dahrendorf, in his book *Reflections on the Revolutions in Europe*, has insisted that the events of 1989 cannot be interpreted simply as an overthrow of communism in favour of capitalism. Rather, they were constitutional revolutions in which freedom was chosen over serfdom. It was not just communism that died in 1989 but, in Dahrendorf's words, 'the belief in a closed world which is governed by a monopoly of "Truth"'.[15]

## The end of the cold war and the collapse of the Soviet Union, 1989–91

Few observers in the West predicted the collapse of the Soviet Union in the late 1980s. Here it is useful to bear in mind De Tocqueville's observation in the nineteenth century that revolutions occur not when dictatorial regimes are at their most repressive but, rather, when they are seeking to reform themselves. This was certainly the case with the Soviet Union under Gorbachev. The Soviet Union was not on the point of collapse when Gorbachev assumed power in 1985; it began to disintegrate as a result of his policies.[16]

One of Gorbachev's greatest weaknesses was his failure to understand the revolutionary potential of the nationalist issue. In 1988 and 1989 Armenians in Karabakh demanded separation from Azerbaijan, Georgia demanded independence from central control and the three Baltic republics of Lithuania, Latvia and Estonia called for independence. Gorbachev was willing to grant greater autonomy to the republics, but his conservative opponents were concerned that his reforming policies would lead to the break-up of the Soviet Union and that was the main reason for the *coup* against him in August 1991.

In fact, Gorbachev believed in 'Soviet man', that is, the existence of a Soviet Union that went beyond national particularities. But, as we have seen in Eastern Europe, revolution engulfed his reforms. At the end of that historic year, 1989, Gorbachev met President Bush at Malta in December and declared: 'We don't consider you an enemy any more'.[17] The Malta summit symbolically represented the end of the cold war.

The ending of the cold war had repercussions on the world outside Europe. The withdrawal of Cuban troops in Angola in 1991 ended the civil war there that had existed since 1975. In 1989 Vietnam, under pressure from the Soviet Union, withdrew its troops from Cambodia. In Central America the withdrawal of Soviet support for Cuba led to a decline in Cuban support for Nicaragua and the rebels in El Salvador and prompted the Sandinista Government in Nicaragua to hold an election in 1990, which brought in a coalition Government. In the Horn of

Africa the war between Ethiopia and Somalia ended when the Soviet Union ended its support for Ethiopia and the United States did the same in Somalia.

It took another year-and-a-half after the end of the cold war for the Soviet Union to collapse. In 1990 East and West Germany were reunited and the division of Europe was at an end. But on this issue, as well as losing Eastern Europe, Gorbachev was on the defensive at home. Gorbachev's main challenger from the left was Boris Yeltsin, who was elected President of the Republic of Russia in June 1991. But the *coup* that overturned Gorbachev in August was engineered by hard-liners. It failed because Yeltsin stood firm and the military refused to join the conspirators. As a result of the failed *coup* the Communist Party was banned after 74 years in power and the Soviet Union itself disintegrated over the next four months, from August to December.

How important was American policy in bringing about the collapse of communism in the Soviet Union? George Kennan, the architect of containment, wrote an article in the *New York Times* in 1992 claiming that the United States simply did not have the power to influence changes within the Soviet Union. But Kennan's own original concept of containment was based on the assumption that containment would 'encourage an internal implosion in the Soviet Union'.[18] Soviet communism did collapse from within and that collapse took place at a time when the United States, under Presidents Reagan and Bush, pursued a policy of firmness towards the Soviet Union. But it is important to bear in mind that the Soviet Union under Gorbachev was working out its own dynamic of reform and revolution, and the timescale for that process was not determined primarily by relations with the United States.

# Conclusion

Fundamentally the cold war was a confrontation between the United States and the Soviet Union, fuelled on both sides by the belief that the ideology of the other side had to be destroyed. In this sense it was a zero-sum game in which co-existence was not possible – one side could win only at the expense of the other. The Soviet Union held to Lenin's belief that conflict between communism and capitalism was 'inevitable'. The United States believed that peace and stability in the world would only emerge when the evil of communism had been exorcised. Each side imputed unlimited objectives to the other. At the ideological level Moscow's Manichean communist world-view, which saw capitalism as an absolute evil, fed off Washington's Manichean world-view, which saw communism as an absolute evil, and in this way each helped to sustain the other's prophecy.

We have seen that the basis of United States foreign policy since 1945 was the doctrine of containment sketched out by George Kennan in the Long Telegram of 1946. Kennan argued that the methods and goals of the United States and Soviet Union were irreconcilable and therefore that the United States should prepare for a long struggle. At some point in the future the 'illegitimate' government of the Soviet Union would collapse from within and the struggle would be over. This is precisely what happened to the Soviet Union under Gorbachev. What is important to note here, however, is not that the United States scored a 'victory', but to understand how it conceived its foreign policy during the cold war.

Containment was a hard-headed, even negative, doctrine in the sense that it argued for the *status quo* and against the strong tendency in the United States to launch a crusade against communism. But it also reflected the utopianism of the United States in the sense that it looked not to the balance of power but to the transformation of Soviet society as the ultimate goal. The American tradition of diplomacy from the time of Woodrow Wilson has been to define its interests in terms of universal principles and values, not territory and national security.[1]

This moralistic strain in United States foreign policy came out strongly in the Truman Doctrine, where the President spoke in Wilsonian terms of the struggle between two ways of life – the free and the totalitarian – and pledged his country to support the former. Even in Korea the United States defended its support for South Korea not in terms of its geopolitical significance but, rather, symbolically in terms of refusing to allow communist aggression to go unopposed. Liberty, not national interest, was the touchstone of American foreign policy.

Because of this ideological way of looking at the world America saw particular events as part of a global communist threat, or even conspiracy. The Czech *coup* (1948), the Berlin Blockade (1948–9), the communist victory in China (1949) and the Korean War (1950–3) were all crucial in confirming the American anti-communist mind-set in the early years of the cold war. In Europe communism was indistinguishable from the power of the Soviet Union. But in Asia communism was often embodied in a secondary power. This was the case in Vietnam. The United States could not see Vietnam in geopolitical terms, but assumed that North Vietnam was controlled by Beijing and that Beijing was controlled in turn by Moscow. Therefore, the defence of South Vietnam became a matter of principle rather than interest, and the United States found it impossible to withdraw without losing face until it was too late.

Nixon was the first president to think about the cold war in more geopolitical terms. At the height of the Vietnam War Nixon and Kissinger took advantage of the Sino–Soviet border clash in 1969 to open up a dialogue with China. While American soldiers were dying on the battlefield in Vietnam Nixon was welcomed in Beijing by Mao Zedong. This amounted to a de-emphasis of ideology and made possible the triangular diplomacy between the Soviet Union, China and the United States of the 1970s. The presidency of Reagan, by contrast, with its references to the 'evil empire' of the Soviet Union, was in many ways a reversion to the Wilsonian tradition of moralism.

By the 1980s, however, it was not what happened in the United States that was important, but what happened in the Soviet Union. The new generation of Soviet leadership under Gorbachev was crucial in bringing about the end of the cold war. Gorbachev remained a socialist, but he rejected the idea of an inevitable world conflict with the West. In doing so he undercut the American policy of containment, which was essentially a reactive stance to the Soviet threat, real or imagined. The decisive events in this process were the revolutions in 1989. The cold war began in Eastern Europe and it ended in Eastern Europe. Once Soviet military power was removed from Eastern Europe, the way was clear to end the division of Europe and, with it, the cold war.

The cold war was an ideological and geopolitical struggle between two opposing systems. Equally important, it was a struggle that took place during the first fifty years of the nuclear age, and the existence of nuclear weapons did much to define the nature of that struggle. The black cloud of nuclear Armageddon hung over the entire cold war period. Yet the bomb was never used in anger after 1945 by either the United States or the Soviet Union. Nuclear weapons certainly exercised a restraining influence on Moscow and Washington and helped to prevent regional conflicts from escalating into a general war. A 'tradition' of non-use became established and grew stronger with each decade of the cold war.[2] The new weapons brought restraint as well as peril.

In spite of the fierce ideological rivalry between the United States and the Soviet Union, the cold war in fact contained strong elements of stability. The very length of the cold war – the longest period of peace in the twentieth century – has led one historian to re-define it as the 'long peace'.[3] Nuclear weapons made people view war as unthinkable for the first time in history, and this fundamental change of attitude influenced the behaviour of the superpowers. Whatever their differences, the Soviet Union and the West shared one common objective –

the prevention of a Third World War. Crises took the place of war in the nuclear age.

The question arises of how order was achieved in a world system without any superior authority. The United Nations clearly failed to perform the role of a supra-national body able to keep the peace. It seems that both Washington and Moscow implicitly accepted certain unwritten sets of rules touching on the following areas: their respective spheres of influence; the avoidance of direct military confrontation; and the non-use of nuclear weapons. With regard to spheres of influence, the United States never seriously attempted to dislodge the Soviet Union from Eastern Europe. The Soviet Union for its part tolerated, without openly approving, United States influence in Western Europe, the Mediterranean, the Middle East and Latin America. In areas where the spheres of influence were left unclear serious crises or actual conflicts were a result. This was the case in West Berlin in 1948, South Korea in 1950 and Cuba in 1962.

The avoidance of direct military confrontation was an objective carefully pursued by each superpower. Three major limited wars were fought by either side after 1945: the United States in Korea and Vietnam and the Soviet Union in Afghanistan. But in none of these wars was there a direct Soviet–American military confrontation. Both sides tended to resort to proxies or indirect means to expand or keep control of an area. The Soviet Union sanctioned the North Korean invasion of South Korea in 1950 without itself becoming directly engaged. In the 1970s the Soviets relied on Cuban troops to promote their interests in sub-Saharan Africa. The United States usually relied on covert influence (the CIA) as the means to defend its sphere of influence.

With regard to nuclear weapons, a tradition of self-deterrence grew up on each side. From time to time both sides publicly declared their willingness to use nuclear weapons in war. But their behaviour told a different story. The United States began to establish a habit of non-use even when it had a clear nuclear monopoly, that is, before 1955. Truman's decision not to use nuclear weapons in the Korean War marked a watershed in the history of international relations in the nuclear age. General MacArthur's call for victory through the use of nuclear weapons was rejected in 1951. From this time onwards the United States and the world learned to live with the idea that victory in a total war was not an option in the nuclear age.

Under Eisenhower's presidency the tradition of non-use of nuclear weapons was confirmed, in spite of the bellicose rhetoric of his Secretary of State, Dulles. Eisenhower rejected Admiral Radford's advice to use atomic weapons to free the French troops from the siege of Dien Bien Phu in 1954. In the crisis over the Taiwan Straits in 1954 Eisenhower made it clear to the People's Republic of China that Taiwan would be defended by nuclear weapons if necessary. But he also made it clear to Chiang Kai-shek that America would not support him in an attack on the mainland. Eisenhower was not averse to making an explicit nuclear threat (for example, in seeking an end to the Korean War), but in specific situations he always found the costs of using them to outweigh the benefits by far.

What about the Soviet Union? The most dangerous moments of the cold war came with the Soviet–American confrontation over Berlin and Cuba in the period 1958–62. Khrushchev sent an ultimatum to the three Western powers occupying West Berlin demanding a change of status for the city in 1958. When the West refused to budge, Khrushchev withdrew his ultimatum. There is every indication that Khrushchev was less willing to risk nuclear war than bluff the West into making changes over Berlin. The story was the same in Cuba four years later. The risk of nuclear war was the main factor restraining both sides. Soviet caution was exercised again in the border crisis of 1969 against China, an opponent with only a small supply of nuclear warheads.

In the 1970s and 1980s Soviet–American relations were dominated by mutual recognition of the need to reach agreement on first limiting, and then reducing, their respective nuclear arsenals. Each side had a vested interest in keeping the nuclear peace. As Gorbachev said in 1987, 'a nuclear tornado will sweep away socialists and capitalists, the just and sinners alike'.[4] As it happened, the cold war ended not with a nuclear explosion, but with the demise of communism in Eastern Europe and the Soviet Union.

# Notes

## Chapter 1

1 Quoted in Thomas (1966), p. 35.
2 Quoted in Gaddis (1978), pp. 148–9.
3 Djilas (1962), p. 90.
4 Ulam (1973), p. 66.
5 Quoted in Hammond (1982), p. 278.
6 Harbutt (1986), p. 169.
7 Yergin (1980), p. 170. This is one of the best accounts of the origins of the cold war. But see also Halle (1967), Gaddis (1972), LaFeber (1993), McCauley (1983), Boyle (1993) and Dunbabin (1994).
8 Kennan (1967), p. 550.
9 Acheson (1969), p. 219.
10 Quoted in Jones (1955), p. 272.
11 Quoted in Ambrose (1985), p. 95.

## Chapter 2

1 White (1978), p. 153.
2 For a colourful account of the Long March see Wilson (1962).
3 Quoted in White (1978), p. 116.
4 Quoted in Lowe (1986), p. 104.
5 Quoted in Ambrose (1985), p. 111.
6 For good discussions of the causes and course of the Korean War see Foot (1985), Lowe (1986) and Hastings (1987).
7 Cumings (1983), p. 55.
8 See Rees (1964) for a thoughtful look at the difficulties that face a liberal society in fighting a limited war.
9 Hastings (1987).

# Chapter 3

1 Quoted in Halle (1967), p. 269.
2 Divine (1981), p. 37.
3 Quoted in Gaddis (1987), p. 129.
4 Quoted in Gaddis (1987), p. 135.
5 On Eisenhower's handling of the Quemoy/Matsu crisis see Ambrose (1984).
6 For standard accounts of Soviet foreign policy see Dallin (1962), Ulam (1974) and Nogee and Donaldson (1984).
7 Mandelbaum (1981), p. 218.
8 Quoted in Wolfe (1970), p. 84.
9 Quoted in Halle (1967), p. 353.
10 On the Berlin crisis of 1961 see the contrasting views of Adomeit (1982) and Shlusser (1973).
11 There is a large literature on the Cuban crisis. For personal accounts see Kennedy (1969) and Schlesinger (1965); for detailed, scholarly treatments see Allison (1971), Garthoff (1989) and Beschloss (1991).

# Chapter 4

1 Quoted in Karnow (1984), p. 20. On George Ball's role as dissenter over Vietnam see Ball (1982) and DiLeo (1991).
2 The literature on Vietnam is enormous. Good narrative accounts are Herring (1979), Karnow (1984) and Short (1989); more analytical are Smith (1968) and Charlton and Moncrieff (1978); very critical of America are Fitzgerald (1984) and Tuchman (1984); less critical are Lewy (1978) and Podhoretz (1983); in a class by itself is the ambitious, moving story told by Sheehan (1989).
3 Quoted in Lewy (1978), p. 12.
4 See Halberstam (1972).
5 Sheehan (1989), p. 287.
6 Herring (1979), p. 124.
7 Kearns (1974), p. 271. For another account of Johnson's role in Vietnam see Schandler (1977).
8 Quoted in Tuchman (1984), p. 449.
9 See McNamara (1995). For a remarkably similar argument to McNamara's see the article by Morgenthau (1968) in Graebner (1977).

# Chapter 5

1 This section draws heavily on Gittings's article in Chomsky (1982).
2 Camilleri (1980), p. 32.
3 See Nogee and Donaldson (1984), pp. 224–32.
4 Yahuda (1983), p. 111.
5 See Mandelbaum (1988), p. 223.
6 See Segal (1982), p. 8.
7 This analogy is taken from Segal (1982).

## Chapter 6

1 The most thorough treatment of détente is in Garthoff (1985). For other useful accounts see Stevenson (1985), Bowker and Williams (1988), Gaddis (1982, 1984), Hyland (1987) and Ashton (1989).
2 Quoted in Nogee and Donaldson (1984), p. 259.
3 Gaddis (1982), p. 277.
4 Gaddis (1984), p. 359.
5 Bowker and Williams (1988), p. 75.
6 Quoted in Bowker and Williams (1988), p. 249.
7 Gaddis (1984), p. 363.

## Chapter 7

1 This section on Reagan's first term as president draws on Blacker (1987) and Garthoff (1985).
2 Quoted in Garthoff (1985), p. 1,013.
3 Freedman (1981), p. 414.
4 Quoted in Garthoff (1985), p. 1,054.
5 Mandelbaum and Talbott (1987), p. 27.
6 See Dibb (1988) and Bialer (1986).
7 For Gorbachev and his 'new thinking' see White (1990), Bialer and Mandelbaum (1988) and Hyland (1987).
8 Quoted in Jacobsen (1989), p. 20.
9 Quoted in Talbott (1988), p. 287.
10 See Doder and Branson (1991).
11 See White (1990).
12 For different assessments of Reagan as president see Mervin (1990) and Hogan (1990).
13 Ash (1990), p. 78.
14 For general background accounts of the revolutions in Eastern Europe see Brown (1991), Hawkes (1990) and Ash (1989).
15 Dahrendorf (1990), p. 37.
16 See Crockatt (1995), p. 341.
17 Quoted in Garthoff (1994), p. 406.
18 Quoted in Crockatt (1995), p. 357.

## Conclusion

1 See Kissinger (1994) for the moralist tradition in American diplomacy.
2 For the best account of the choices about the bomb that the two superpowers had to face in the cold war see Bundy (1988).
3 Gaddis (1987). The discussion of nuclear self-deterrence draws heavily on this book.
4 Quoted in Bundy (1988), p. 593.

# Select bibliography

Acheson, D. (1969) *Present at the Creation: My Years in the State Department* (New York)

Adomeit, H. (1982) *Soviet Risk-Taking and Crisis Behaviour* (London)

Allison, G.T. (1971) *Essence of Decision, Explaining the Cuban Missile Crisis* (Boston)

Alperovitz, G. (1965) *Atomic Diplomacy* (London)

Ambrose, S. (1984) *Eisenhower the President*, Vol. 2, *1952–69* (London)

Ambrose, S. (1985) *Rise to Globalism: American Foreign Policy Since 1938* (London)

Ash, T.G. (1989) *The Uses of Adversity* (Cambridge)

Ash, T.G. (1990) *We The People, The Revolution of '89* (Cambridge)

Ashton, S.R. (1989) *In Search of Détente* (London)

Ball, G. (1982) *The Past Has Another Pattern* (New York)

Beschloss, M. (1991) *Kennedy v. Khrushchev: The Crisis Years 1960–63* (London)

Bialer, S. (1986) *The Soviet Paradox: External Expansion, Internal Decline* (New York)

Bialer, S. and Mandelbaum, M. (1988) *The Global Rivals* (London)

Blacker, C.D. (1987) *Reluctant Warriors: The United States, Soviet Union and Arms Control* (New York)

Bowker, M. and Williams, P. (1988) *Superpower Détente: A Reappraisal* (London)

Bown, C. and Mooney, P. (1989) *Cold War to Détente* (London)

Boyle, P.G. (1993) *American-Soviet Relations* (London)

Brown, J.F. (1991) *Surge to Freedom: The End of Communist Rule in Eastern Europe* (Chapel Hill)

Brzezinski, Z. (1989) *The Grand Failure: The Birth and Death of Communism in the Twentieth Century* (New York)

Bundy, M. (1988) *Danger and Survival: Choices About the Bomb in the First Fifty Years* (New York)

Camilleri, J. (1980) *Chinese Foreign Policy, The Maoist Era and its Aftermath* (New York)

Charlton, M. and Moncrieff, A. (1978) *Many Reasons Why* (London)

Charlton, M. (1984) *The Eagle and the Small Birds* (London)

Crockatt, R. (1995) *The Fifty Years War: The United States and the Soviet Union in World Politics, 1941–91* (London)

Cumings, B. (ed.) (1983) *Child of Conflict, The Korean–American Relationship* (Washington, DC)

Dahrendorf, R. (1990) *Reflections on the Revolutions in Europe* (London)

Dallin, D.J. (1962) *Soviet Foreign Policy after Stalin* (Philadelphia)

Dibb, P. (1988) *The Soviet Union: The Incomplete Superpower* (London)

DiLeo, D. (1991) *George Ball, Vietnam and the Rethinking of Containment* (Chapel Hill)

Divine, R.A. (1981) *Eisenhower and the Cold War* (Oxford)

Djilas, M. (1962) *Conversations with Stalin* (London)

Doder, D. and Branson, L. (1991) *Gorbachev, Heretic in the Kremlin* (New York)

Dunbabin, J.P.D. (1994) *The Cold War: The Great Powers and Their Allies* (London)

Fitzgerald, F. (1984) *Fire in the Lake* (New York)

Foot, R. (1985) *The Wrong War: American Policy and the Dimensions of the Korean Conflict, 1950–53* (Ithaca)

Freedman, L. (1981) *The Evolution of Nuclear Strategy* (London)

Gaddis, J.L. (1972) *The United States and the Origins of the Cold War, 1941–1947* (New York)

Gaddis, J.L. (1978) *Russia, the Soviet Union and the United States: An Interpretative History* (New York)

Gaddis, J.L. (1982) *Strategies of Containment* (New York)

Gaddis, J.L. (1984) 'The Rise, Fall and Decline of Détente', *Foreign Affairs*, 62

Gaddis, J.L. (1987) *The Long Peace: Inquiries into the History of the Cold War* (Oxford)

Garthoff, R. (1985) *Détente and Confrontation: American–Soviet Relations, Nixon to Reagan* (Washington, DC)

Garthoff, R. (1989) *Reflections on the Cuban Missile Crisis* (Washington, DC)

Garthoff, R. (1994) *The Great Transition: American–Soviet Relations and the End of the Cold War* (Washington, DC)

Gittings, J. (1974) *The World and China, 1922–1972* (London)

Gittings, J. (1982) 'China: Half a Superpower', in Chomsky, N. *et al.* (1982) *Superpowers in Collision* (London)

Halberstam, D. (1972) *The Best and the Brightest* (New York)

Halle, L. (1967) *The Cold War as History* (New York)

Halliday, F. (1983) *The Making of the Second Cold War* (London)

Hammond, T. (ed.) (1982) *Witnesses to the Origins of the Cold War* (Washington, DC)

Harbutt, F.J. (1986) *The Iron Curtain* (Oxford)

Hastings, M. (1987) *The Korean War* (London)

Hawkes, N. (ed.) (1990) *Tearing Down the Curtain: The People's Revolution in Eastern Europe* (London)

Herring, G. (1979) *America's Longest War: The United States and Vietnam, 1950–1975* (New York)

Hogan, J. (ed.) (1990) *The Reagan Years: The Record in Presidential Leadership* (Manchester)

Hogan, M.J. (ed.) (1992) *The End of the Cold War: Its Meaning and Implications* (Cambridge)

Hyland, W.G. (1987) *Mortal Rivals: Understanding the Hidden Pattern of Soviet–American Relations* (New York)

Hyland, W.G. (1990) *The Cold War is Over* (New York)

Jacobsen, C.G. (ed.) (1989) *Soviet Foreign Policy* (London)

Jones, J.M. (1955) *The Fifteen Weeks* (New York)

Karnow, S. (1984) *Vietnam: A History* (London)

Kearns, D. (1974) *Lyndon Johnson and the American Dream* (London)

Kennan, G.F. (1967) *Memoirs, 1925–1950* (New York)

Kennedy, R.F. (1969) *Thirteen Days: A Memoir of the Cuban Missile Crisis* (New York)

Kissinger, H. (1994) *Diplomacy* (New York)

LaFeber, W. (1993) *America, Russia and the Cold War, 1945–1992* (New York)

Lewy, G. (1978) *America and Vietnam* (Oxford)

Lowe, P. (1986) *Origins of the Korean War* (London)

McCauley, M. (1983) *Origins of the Cold War, 1945–49* (London)

McNamara, R. (1995) *In Retrospect: The Tragedy and Lessons of Vietnam* (New York)

Mandelbaum, M. (1979) *The Nuclear Question: The United States and Nuclear Weapons, 1946–1976* (Cambridge)

Mandelbaum, M. (1981) *The Nuclear Revolution: International Politics Before and After Hiroshima* (Cambridge)

Mandelbaum, M. (1988) *The Fate of Nations* (Cambridge)

Mandelbaum, M. and Talbott, S. (1987) *Reagan and Gorbachev* (New York)

Mervin, D. (1990) *Ronald Reagan and the American Presidency* (London)

Morgenthau, H.J. (1968) 'US Misadventure in Vietnam', in Graebner, N. (1977) *Cold War Diplomacy, American Foreign Policy, 1945–1975* (New York)

Nitze, P.H. (1989) *From Hiroshima to Glasnost* (New York)

Nogee, J. and Donaldson, R. (1984) *Soviet Foreign Policy Since World War II* (London)

Oberdorfer, D. (1992) *The Turn: From the Cold War to a New Era* (New York)

Partos, G. (1993) *The World That Came in From the Cold: Perspectives from East and West on the Cold War* (London)

Podhoretz, N. (1983) *Why We Were in Vietnam* (New York)

Rees, D. (1964) *Korea: The Limited War* (London)

Schandler, H.Y. (1977) *The Unmaking of a President: Lyndon Johnson and Vietnam* (Princeton)

Schlesinger, A. (1965) *A Thousand Days* (London)

Schlesinger, A. (1967) 'The Origins of the Cold War', *Foreign Affairs*, 46

Segal, G. (ed.) (1982) *The China Factor: Peking and the Superpowers* (London)

Sheehan, N. (1989) *A Bright Shining Lie: John Paul Vann and America in Vietnam* (London)

Shlusser, R. (1973) *The Berlin Crisis of 1961* (New York)

Short, A. (1989) *The Origins of the Vietnam War* (London)

Shultz, G. (1993) *Turmoil and Triumph: My Years as Secretary of State* (New York)

Stevenson, R.W. (1985) *The Rise and Fall of Détente: Relaxation of Tension in US–Soviet Relations, 1953–84* (London)

Smith, R. (1968) *Vietnam and the West* (London)

Talbott, S. (1988) *The Master of the Game: Paul Nitze and the Nuclear Peace* (New York)

Thomas, H. (1986) *The Armed Truce: The Beginnings of the Cold War, 1945–46* (London)

Tuchman, B. (1984) *The March of Folly* (London)

Ulam, A. (1973) *The Rivals: America and Russia since World War II* (London)

Ulam, A. (1974) *Expansion and Coexistence: The History of Soviet Foreign Relations* (New York)

Ulam, A. (1983) *Dangerous Relations: The Soviet Union in World Politics, 1970–1983* (Oxford)

Walker, M. (1993) *The Cold War and the Making of the Modern World* (London)

White, S. (1990) *Gorbachev in Power* (Cambridge)

White, T.H. (1946) *Thunder Out of China* (New York)

White, T.H. (1978) *In Search of History* (New York)

Wilson, D. (1962) *The Long March* (London)

Wolfe, T.W. (1970) *Soviet Power and Europe, 1945–1970* (London)

Yahuda, M. (1983) *Towards the End of Isolationism: China's Foreign Policy after Mao* (London)

Yergin, D. (1980) *Shattered Peace: The Origins of the Cold War and the National Security State* (London)

Young, J.W. (1993) *Cold War and Détente, 1941–91* (London)